debbie bliss
the **baby knits** book

the ultimate collection of
knitwear designs for newborns to 3-year-olds

Trafalgar Square Publishing

For my very special friend
Patsy and her mother Isabel

First published in the United States of
America in 2002 by
Trafalgar Square Publishing
North Pomfret, Vermont 05053

**Printed and bound in Singapore
by Tien Wah Press**

Editor: Sally Harding
Designers: Maggie Town and Beverly Price
Photographer: Sandra Lousada
Stylist: Sammie Bell
Pattern checker: Rosy Tucker
Charts: Anthony Duke

ISBN 1-57076-234-1

Colour separation by Colorlito, Milan

Library of Congress Catalog Card Number:
2002108046

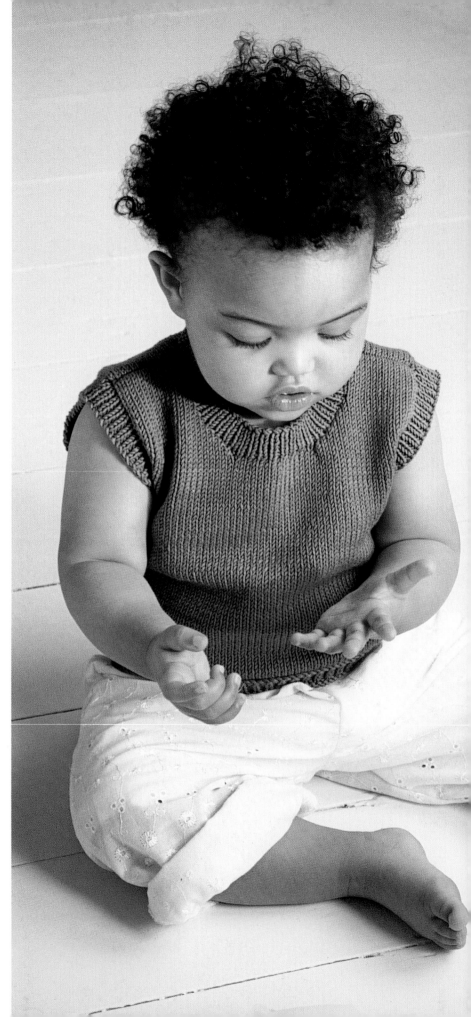

contents

introduction

There is always something very special about knitting for babies and children—nothing can compare to the message and unique quality that hand-knitted garments hold.

The Baby Knits Book is divided into Simple, Cosy and Special. The Simple chapter includes easy knits for the beginner and for those, like new mothers, who do not have much time on their hands. The designs here are worked in basic stitches and classic styles—a soft cashmere-mix jacket and top, a throw, luxurious and gentle enough to wrap against a baby's skin, a kimono and a tank top. The Cosy chapter has generous sweaters to snuggle into, outdoor sporty knits for active children, and a bear in a lamb suit to cuddle up to. In the Special section, jackets and shoes are embellished with embroidery and beads, perfect for gifts, and there is an heirloom alphabet blanket to be cherished for years.

All the designs have been knitted in my own range of yarns, which have been especially selected not only for their baby-friendly handle but for their easy wash and wear as well. The collection has also been put together to reflect the range of knitting skills, from the basic to the more advanced.

designing for children

There are certain points I always try to keep in mind when I am designing for babies and children. I tend to produce cardigans rather than sweaters for small babies as they dislike having garments pulled over their heads, and it can be difficult to dress them when they are too small to sit up. If I am working on a sweater design for this age I will introduce a shoulder fastening, an envelope neck, or a front or back neck opening. Another practical style is a ballerina, cross-over style that avoids buttons, as they can be uncomfortable when babies roll on to their tummies. I will only use yarn that I know is soft and kind to babies' skin.

Older children can be more of a challenge. I believe that we often have to use all our powers of persuasion to encourage them to wear hand knits. They have been brought up in a world of fleeces, sweatshirts and man-made fibers, and they are used to wearing fabrics that move with them and are light, soft and comfortable. With this thought uppermost, I allow plenty of ease in the garments, especially at the underarm, and particularly if they are worked in a very textured pattern such as an Aran, which produces a denser and less elastic fabric.

I always quote the actual measurements of the garments and the age of the wearer rather than the chest measurement. This is because from personal experience although I could always remember the age of my children, I floundered when it came to knowing the chest size! The chest size can also be rather a red herring–all designs, unless they are very tightly fitting fashion garments for an adult, have ease. Ease is the extra measurement allowed for comfort and movement, and also to create a particular style, such as a generous outerwear cabled sweater. Some readers have queried the quoted measurements on my children's designs because they are comparing adults' chest measurements with the actual measurements of a child's garment. I usually ask them to measure an existing garment that the child they are knitting for wears, and they can be surprised to find that they match up closely to the measurements in the pattern. I also like to think that the time and money, not to mention love, that has been invested into knitting the design should be rewarded by having a knit that will see the child through at least a couple of years, even if a rather larger than is strictly needed garment is produced originally. However, if the reader is not happy with my measurements I will always suggest that they knit a smaller or larger size.

Try to involve the child in the design you are knitting for them rather than just produce one in the colors or style you like! It is a wonderful opportunity to teach them from an early age that not all their clothes just appear by magic in shops, that they can be lovingly made especially for them. It is also a great way to introduce them to the craft and to looking at colors and textures. Even choosing buttons can be fun.

Debbie Bliss

basic information

Following pattern instructions

Figures for larger sizes are given in parentheses ( ). Where only one figure appears, this applies to all sizes. Work the figures given in brackets [ ] the number of times stated afterwards. Where 0 appears, no stitches or rows are worked for this size. As you follow the pattern, make sure that you are consistently using the right stitches for your size–it is only too easy to switch sizes inside the brackets. One way to avoid this is to go through the instructions first and mark off the size you are knitting with a colored marker or highlighter.

The quantities of yarn quoted in the instructions are based on the yarn used by the knitter for the original garment and amounts should therefore be considered approximate. A slight variation in gauge can make the difference between using less or more yarn than that stated in the pattern. Before buying the yarn look at the measurements in the knitting patterns to be sure which size you want to knit. My patterns quote the actual finished size of the garment, not the chest size of the wearer. The length of the garment is taken from the shoulder shaping to the cast-on edge.

Gauge

Each pattern in the book states a gauge–the number of stitches and rows per inch or centimeter that should be obtained with the given needles, yarn and stitch pattern. Check your gauge carefully before starting work. A slight variation in gauge can spoil the look of a garment and alter the proportions that the designer wanted. A too loose gauge will produce uneven knitting and an unstable fabric that can droop or lose its shape after washing, whilst too tight a gauge can create a hard, unforgiving fabric.

To make a guage square use the same needles, yarn and stitch pattern quoted in the guage note in the pattern. Knit a sample at least 5in/12.5cm square. Smooth out the finished sample on a flat surface but do not stretch it. To check the stitch gauge place a tape measure horizontally on the sample and mark 4in/10cm with pins. Count the number of stitches between pins. To check the row gauge place the tape measure vertically on the sample and mark 4in/10cm. Count the number of rows between the pins. If the number of stitches and rows is greater than that stated in the pattern, try again using larger needles. If the number of stitches and rows is less, use smaller needles. If you are only able to obtain either the stitch or the row gauge, it is the stitch gauge that is the most important to get right, as the length of many patterns are calculated by measurement rather than the amount or rows you need to work to achieve it.

Garment care

Taking care of your knitted garments is important. If you have invested all that time and labor into knitting them, you want them to look good for as long as possible. Follow these guidelines for the best results.

Check the yarn label for washing instructions. Most yarns can now be machine washed on a delicate wool cycle. Prior to washing, make a note of the measurements of the garment, such as the width and length. After washing, lay the garment flat and check the measurements again to see if they are the same. If not, smooth and pat it back into shape.

Some knitters prefer to hand wash their garments. Use soap flakes specially created for hand knits, and warm rather

Needle conversion chart

This needle conversion chart covers all the knitting needle sizes used for the patterns in this book.

US sizes	UK metric
size 2	2¾mm
size 2-3	3mm
size 3	3¼mm
size 5	3¾mm
size 6	4mm
size 7	4½mm
size 8	5mm

Standard abbreviations

alt = alternate
beg = begin(ning)
cont = continu(e)ing
dec = decreas(e)ing
foll = following
inc = increas(e)ing
k = knit
m1 = make one by picking up the loop lying between st just worked and next st and working into back of it
patt = pattern
p = purl
psso = pass slipped st over
rem = remain(ing)
rep = repeat(ing)
skpo = slip 1, knit 1, pass slipped stitch over
sl = slip
st(s) = stitch(es)
st st = stockinette stitch
tbl = through back loop
tog = together
yf = yarn forward
yon = yarn over needle
yrn = yarn around needle

than hot water. Handle the knits gently in the water – do not rub or wring, as this can felt the fabric. Rinse well to get rid of any soap, and squeeze out excess water. You may need to get rid of more water by rolling the garment in a towel, or you can use the delicate spin cycle of the washing machine. Dry the garment by laying it out flat on top of a towel to absorb moisture, and smooth and pat into shape. Do not dry knits near direct heat such as a radiator. Store your knits loosely folded to allow the air to circulate.

types of yarns

Fibers are divided into two main categories, natural and synthetic. Natural fibers are then divided into animal fibers –wool, angora, cashmere, silk, etc.–and those from vegetable fibers such as cotton, linen, and hemp. This is a guide to the yarns used in this book.

Wool

Wool spun from the fleece of sheep is the yarn that is the most commonly associated with knitting. It has many excellent qualities, as it is durable, elastic, and warm in the winter. Wool yarn is particularly good for working color patterns, as the fibers adhere and help prevent the gaps that can appear in Fair Isle or intarsia.

Some knitters find that a simple stitch such as seed stitch or garter stitch can look neater when worked in a wool rather than a cotton yarn.

Cotton

Cotton yarn, made from a natural plant fiber, is an ideal all-seasons yarn, as it is warm in the winter and cool in the summer. I particularly love to work in cotton because it gives a clarity of stitch that shows up subtle stitch patterning such as a seed stitch border on a collar or cuffs.

Cotton and wool

Knitting in yarn that is a blend of wool and cotton is particularly good for children's wear. This is because the wool fibers give elasticity for comfort and the cotton content is perfect for children who find wool irritating against the skin.

Cashmere

Cashmere is made from the underhair of a particular Asian goat. It is associated with the ultimate in luxury, and is unbelievably soft to the touch. If combined with merino wool and microfiber, as in my cashmerino yarn range, it is perfect for babies.

Silk

Silk is a fiber produced by certain caterpillars as they spin their cocoon. Combined with cotton, as in my cotton/silk range, it can make beautiful yarn that also has hardwearing qualities.

buying yarn

Always try to buy the yarn quoted in the knitting pattern. The designer will have created the design specifically with that yarn in mind and a substitute may produce a garment that is different from the original. For instance, the design may rely for its appeal on a subtle stitch pattern that is lost when using a yarn of an inferior quality, or a synthetic when used to replace a natural yarn such as cotton will create a limp fabric and the crispness of the original design lost. We cannot accept responsibility for the finished product if any yarn other than the one specified is used.

If you do decide to use a substitute yarn, buy a yarn that is the same weight and where possible the same fiber content. It is essential to use a yarn that has the same gauge as the original or the measurements will change. You should also check yardage or meterage–yarn that weighs the same may have different lengths so you may need to buy more or less yarn. Check the ball band on the yarn. Most yarn labels now carry all the information you need about fiber content, washing instructions, weight and yardage or meterage.

It is essential to check the dye lot number on the yarn label. Yarns are dyed in batches or lots, which can sometimes vary quite considerably. Your retailer may not have the same dye lot later on, so it is worth trying to buy all your yarn for a project at the same time. If you know that sometimes you use more yarn than that quoted in the pattern, buy more. If it is not possible to buy the amount you need all in the same dye lot, work the borders or the lower edges in the odd one since the color change is less likely to show here.

debbie bliss yarns

The following are descriptions of my yarns and a guide to their weights and types. All the yarns used in the designs are machine washable. (See page 128 for yarn distributors.)

Debbie Bliss merino double knitting: a 100% merino wool in a double-knitting weight. Soft to the touch but hardwearing. Approximately 120yds/110m/50g/2oz ball.

Debbie Bliss merino aran: a 100% merino wool in an Aran or fisherman weight. Ideal for outerwear. Approximately 85yds/78m/50g/2oz ball.

Debbie Bliss wool/cotton: a 50% merino wool, 50% cotton lightweight yarn that is between a 4-ply and a double knitting. This yarn combines the crispness of cotton with the elasticity of wool. Approximately 117yds/107m/50g/2oz ball.

Debbie Bliss cashmerino aran: a 55% merino wool, 33% microfiber, 12% cashmere yarn in an Aran or fisherman weight. A luxurious yarn with a beautiful handle. Approximately 98yds/90m/50g/2oz ball.

Debbie Bliss baby cashmerino: a 55% merino wool, 33% microfiber, 12% cashmere lightweight yarn between a 4-ply and a double knitting. It is perfect for knitting for newborn and small babies as it is gentle against the skin. Approximately 137yds/125m/50g/2oz ball.

Debbie Bliss cotton double knitting: a 100% cotton yarn in a double-knitting weight. It knits up smoothly, showing up stitch detail well. Approximately 92yds/84m/50g/2oz ball.

Debbie Bliss cotton/silk: a 80% cotton, 20% silk yarn in an Aran weight. It has the crispness of cotton with a slight sheen. Approximately 69yds/63m/50g/2oz ball.

simple

coathanger

The easiest of makes, this seed stitch coathanger has a contrasting edge and is trimmed with a pretty bow. It is a great first project for a beginner.

Materials
One 50g/2oz ball of Debbie Bliss cotton double knitting in Main shade (M) and small amount in Contrast shade (C).
Pair of US 6(4mm) knitting needles.
Small amount of wadding.
12in/30cm wooden coathanger.
12in/30cm narrow ribbon.

Gauge
20 sts and 30 rows to 4in/10cm over seed st using US 6(4mm) needles.

Abbreviations See page 7.

To make
With US 6(4mm) needles and C, cast on 61 sts.
K 4 rows.
Change to M.
K 1 row.
Next row K1, * p1, k1; rep from * to end.
This row forms seed st.
Cont in seed st until work measures 4½in/11cm from beg, ending with a right side row.
K 1 row.
Change to C.
K 4 rows.
Bind off.

Finish
Lightly pad the hanger with wadding. Place knitting around the hanger and stitch together cast on and bind off edges. Sew up side seams. Tie ribbon in a bow around hanger neck.

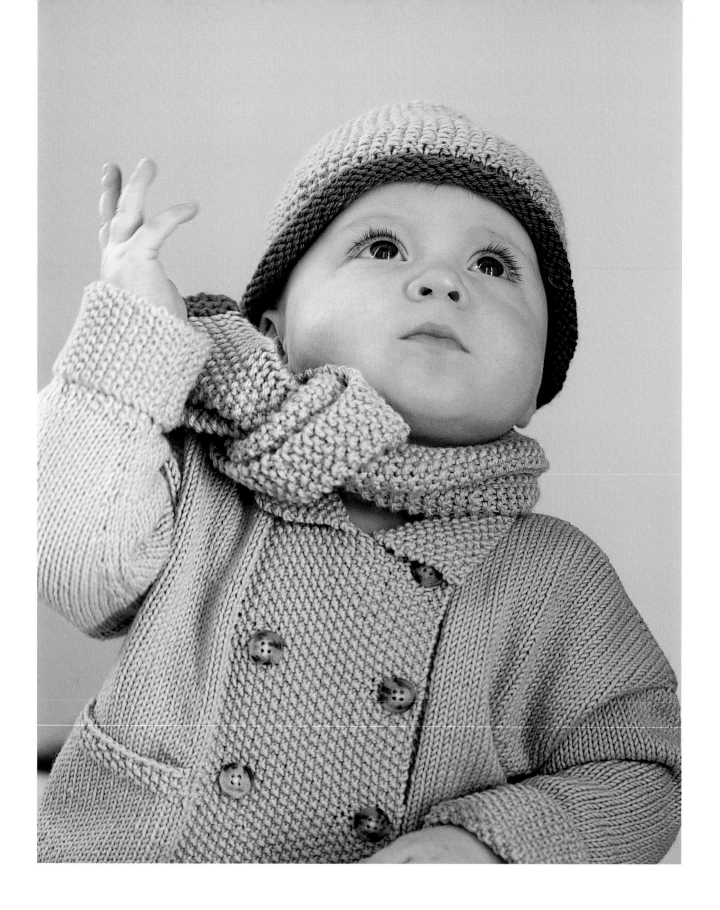

seed stitch hat, scarf, and throw

Knitted in reversible seed stitch and worked in a cashmere mix, the hat and scarf are an ideal gift set for a new knitter to make for a new baby. The baby blanket is a perfect size for a small pram or buggy.

Measurements

Hat and scarf:

To fit ages	3-6 mths
Scarf length	23in/59cm
Scarf width	4¼in/11cm

Throw:
Approximately 22 x 29in/56 x 74cm.

Materials

Hat: One 50g/2oz ball of Debbie Bliss cashmerino aran in Main shade (M) and small amount in Contrast shade (C). Pair of US 8(5mm) knitting needles.

Scarf: Two 50g/2oz balls of Debbie Bliss cashmerino aran in Main shade (M) and small amount in Contrast shade (C). Pair each of US 7(4½mm) and US 8(5mm) knitting needles.

Throw: Six 50g/2oz balls of Debbie Bliss cashmerino aran in Main shade (M) and two balls in Contrast shade (C). Pair each of US 7(4½mm) and US 8(5mm) knitting needles.

Gauge

20 sts and 36 rows to 4in/10cm square over seed st using US 8(5mm) needles.

Abbreviations See page 7.

Note When changing colors on Throw, twist yarns together on the wrong side to avoid holes.

Hat

With US 8(5mm) needles and C, cast on 72 sts.

Beg with a k row, work 5 rows in st st.

Change to M.

P 1 row.

1st row [K1, p1] to end.

2nd row [P1, k1] to end.

These 2 rows form seed st.

Cont in seed st until work measures 5in/13cm from cast on edge, ending with a wrong side row.

Shape top

Next row [Seed st 6, work 3tog] to end. 56 sts.

Work 3 rows.

Next row [Seed st 4, work 3tog] to end. 40 sts.

Work 3 rows.

Next row [Seed st 2, work 3tog] to end. 24 sts.

Work 1 row.

Next row [Work 3tog] to end. 8 sts.

Break yarn, leaving a long end. Thread through rem sts, pull up and secure. Join seam, reversing seam on contrast roll.

Scarf

With US 7(4½mm) needles and C, cast on 21 sts.

K 4 rows.

Change to US 8(5mm) needles and M.

K 1 row.

Next row K3, * p1, k1; rep from * to last 4 sts, p1, k3.

Rep the last row until work measures 23in/58cm from cast on edge, ending with a wrong side row.

Change to US 7(4½mm) needles and C.

K 4 rows.

Bind off.

Throw

With US 7(4½mm) and C, cast on 113 sts.

K 4 rows.

Change to US 8(5mm) needles.

Next row K3C, k with M to last 3 sts, k3C.

Next row K3C, * k1M, p1M; rep from * to last 4 sts, k1M, k3C.

Rep the last row, working seed st in M with k3C at each end of every row, until work measures 28in/72cm, ending with a wrong side row.

Next row With C, k to end.

Change to US 7(4½mm) needles.

K 4 rows in C.

Bind off.

seed stitch hat, scarf, and throw   **17**

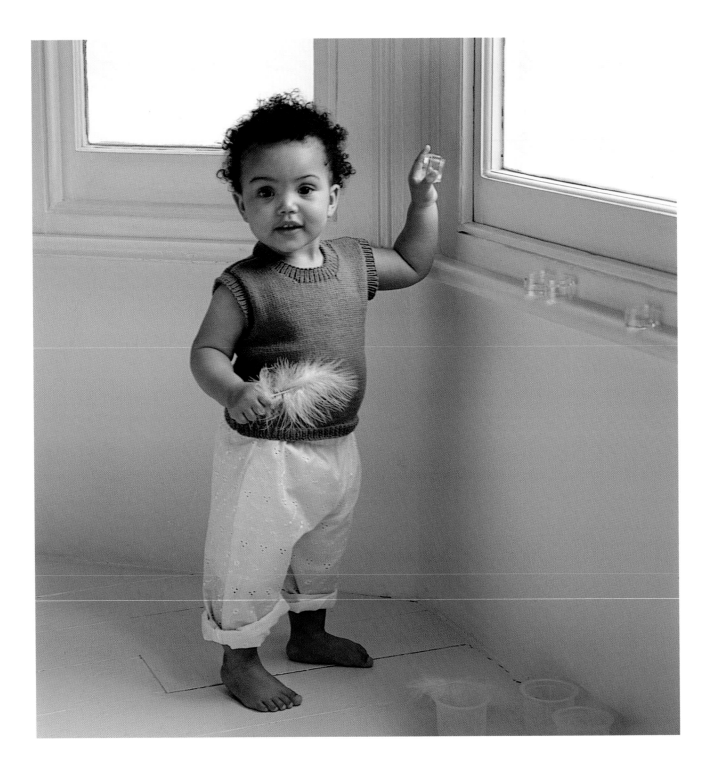

tank top

Knitted in stockinette stitch with a wool and cotton mix, this sleeveless summer top is a stylish alternative to the classic T-shirt.

Measurements

To fit ages

3-6	6-9	9-12	12-24	24-36	mths

Actual measurements

Chest

17¾	19¼	21	22¾	24¾	in
45	49	53	58	63	cm

Length to shoulder

8¾	9½	10¼	11¾	13½	in
22	24	26	30	34	cm

Materials

2(2:3:3:3) 50g/2oz balls of Debbie Bliss wool/cotton.
Pair each of US 2(3mm) and US 3 (3¼mm) knitting needles.

Gauge

25 sts and 34 rows to 4in/10cm square over st st using US 3(3¼mm) needles.

Abbreviations See page 7.

Back

With US 2(3mm) needles cast on 58(64:68:74:80) sts.
Rib row * K1, p1; rep from * to end.
Rep the rib row 3(3:5:5:7) times more.
Change to US 3(3¼mm) needles.
Beg with a k row, work in st st until back measures 4¾(5:5½:6¾:8)in/12(13:14:17:20)cm from cast on edge, ending with a p row.
Shape armholes
Bind off 3(4:4:5:5) sts at beg of next 2 rows.
Dec one st at each end of the next and 3(3:4:4:5) foll alt rows. 44(48:50:54:58) sts.
Cont in st st until back measures 8(8¾:9½:11:12½)in/20(22:24:28:32)cm from cast on edge, ending with a p row.
Shape neck
Next row K15(16:17:18:19) sts, turn and work on these sts for first side of back neck.
Dec one st at neck edge on next 4 rows. 11(12:13:14:15) sts.
Work 3 rows. Bind off.
With right side facing, slip center 14(16:16:18:20) sts onto a holder, rejoin yarn to rem sts, k to end.
Complete to match first side of neck shaping.

Front

Work as given for Back until front measures 6¼(7:8:9:10½)in/16(18:20:23:27)cm from cast on edge, ending with a p row.
Shape neck
Next row K17(18:19:20:21) sts, turn and work on these sts for first side of front neck.

Dec one st at neck edge on next and every foll alt row until 11(12:13:14:15) sts rem.

Work straight until front measures same as Back to shoulder, ending with a p row.

Bind off.

With right side facing, slip center 10(12:12:14:16) sts onto a holder, rejoin yarn to rem sts, k to end.

Complete to match first side of neck shaping.

Neckband

Join right shoulder seam.

With right side facing and US 2(3mm) needles, pick up and k20(20:20:22:22) sts down left side of front neck, k across 10(12:12:14:16) sts from front neck holder, pick up and k20(20:20:22:22) sts up right side of front neck, 10 sts down right back neck, k across 14(16:16:18:20) sts from back neck holder, pick up and k10 sts up left back neck. 84(88:88:96:100) sts.

Work 4(4:4:6:6) rows in rib as given for Back.

Bind off in rib.

Armbands

Join left shoulder and neckband seam.

With right side facing and US 2(3mm) needles, pick up and k60(68:72:80:86) sts around armhole edge.

Work 4(4:4:6:6) rows in rib as given for Back.

Bind off in rib.

Finish

Join side and armband seams.

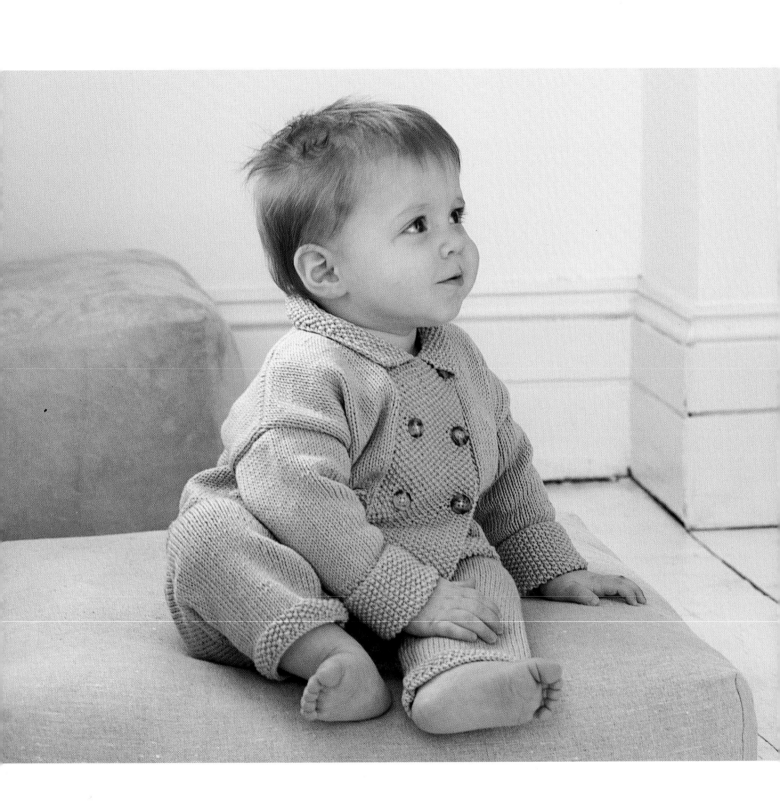

double-breasted jacket and leggings

Measurements

Jacket: To fit ages

3-6	6-12	12-18	18-24	mths

Actual measurements

Chest

23½	25½	27½	29½	in
60	65	70	75	cm

Length

10¼	11¾	13¾	15¼	in
26	30	35	39	cm

Sleeve seam (with cuff turned back)

5½	7	8	8½	in
14	18	20	22	cm

Leggings:

To fit ages	3-6	6-12	mths

Actual measurements

Width	21¼	25½	in
	54	64	cm
Length	11½	14½	in
	29	37	cm
Inside leg seam	4¾	6¾	in
	12	17	cm

Materials

Jacket: 5(6:7:8) 50g/2oz balls Debbie Bliss wool/cotton. Pair each of US 2(2¾mm) and US 3(3¼mm) knitting needles.
6(8:10:10) buttons.
Leggings: 3(3) 50g/2oz balls of Debbie Bliss wool/cotton. Pair each of US 2(2¾mm) and US 3(3¼mm) knitting needles.
Waist length of ½in/1cm wide elastic.

Gauge

25 sts and 34 rows to 4in/10cm square over st st using US 3(3¼mm) needles.

Abbreviations See page 7.

This smart outfit has been designed in the style of a 1950s' baby carriage set. The jacket has a double-breasted fastening and a half belt at the back. This is for the busy rather than the new knitter.

JACKET
Back

With US 3(3¼mm) needles cast on 75(81:87:93) sts.
Seed st row K1, * p1, k1; rep from * to end.
Rep this row 4(4:4:6) times more.
Beg with a k row, work in st st until back measures 10¼(11¾:13¾:15¼)in/26(30:35:39)cm from cast on edge, ending with a p row.
Shape shoulders
Bind off 13(14:15:16) sts at beg of next 4 rows.
Bind off rem 23(25:27:29) sts.

Pocket Linings (make 2)

With US 3(3¼mm) needles cast on 17(19:23:23) sts.
Beg with a k row, work 20 rows in st st.
Leave sts on a holder.

Right Front

With US 3(3¼mm) needles cast on 49(53:57:59) sts.
Work 5(5:5:7) rows in seed st as given for Back.
Next row (right side) Seed st 21(23:25:27), k to end.
Next row P28(30:32:32), seed st to end.
These two rows set the position of the st st with seed st front panel.
Work a further 26(28:28:30) rows.
Place pocket
Next row (right side) Seed st 21(23:25:27), k1, slip next 17(19:23:23) sts onto a holder, k across 17(19:23:23) sts of first pocket lining, k to end.

Work 13(5:7:1) rows.

** **1st buttonhole row** (right side) Seed st 3, bind off 2, seed st next 9(11:13:15), bind off 2, seed st next 3, k to end.

2nd buttonhole row P28(30:32:32), seed st 4, cast on 2, seed st 10(12:14:16), cast on 2, seed st 3.

Work 26(20:26:20) rows. **

Rep from ** to ** 0(1:1:2) times more.

1st buttonhole row (right side) Seed st 3, bind off 2, seed st next (11:13:15), bind off 2, seed st next 3, k to end.

2nd buttonhole row P(30:32:32), seed st 4, cast on 2, seed st (12:14:16), cast on 2, seed st 3.

Work 2 rows, so ending with a wrong side row.

Shape neck

Next row Bind off 18 sts in seed st, patt to end.

Dec one st at neck edge of next 5(7:9:9) rows. 26(28:30:32) sts.

Work straight until right front matches Back to shoulder, ending at side edge.

Shape shoulder

Next row Bind off 13(14:15:16) sts.

Work 1 row. Bind off rem 13(14:15:16) sts.

Left Front

Work as given for Right Front, omitting buttonholes, reversing shapings and placing pocket as follows:

Next row (right side) K10(10:8:8), slip next 17(19:23:23) sts onto a holder, k across 17(19:23:23) sts of second pocket lining, k1, seed st 21(23:25:27).

Sleeves

With US 3(3¼mm) needles cast on 37(39:43:45) sts.

Work 21 rows in seed st as given for Right Front.

Change to US 2(2¾mm) needles and work a further 21 rows in seed st.

Change to US 3(3¼mm) needles.

Beg with a k row, work in st st.

Inc one st at each end of 3rd and every foll 5th row until there are 47(51:61:67) sts.

Cont straight until sleeve measures 7½(9:10:10¼)in/ 19(23:25:27)cm from cast on edge. Bind off.

Collar

Join shoulder seams.

With right side facing, US 2(2¾mm) needles and beg 11 sts in from right front edge, pick up and k23(24:26:28) sts up right front neck to shoulder, 29(31:33:35) sts across back neck, 23(24:26:28) sts down left front neck, ending 11 sts in from left front edge. 75(79:85:91) sts.

Work 1 row in seed st as given for Right Front.

Next 2 rows Seed st to last 23 sts, turn.

Next 2 rows Seed st to last 19 sts, turn.

Next 2 rows Seed st to last 15 sts, turn.

Next 2 rows Seed st to last 11 sts, turn.

Next row Seed st to end.

Seed st 5 rows across all sts.

Change to US 3(3¼mm) needles.

Seed st 12 rows.

Bind off in seed st.

Back Belt

With US 3(3¼mm) needles cast on 53(59:65:71) sts.

Work 9 rows in seed st as given for Back.

Bind off in seed st.

Pocket Tops

With right side facing, slip 17(19:23:23) sts from first pocket holder onto US 2(2¾mm) needles. Work 5 rows in seed st as given for Back.

Bind off in seed st.

Repeat for second pocket.

Finish

Catch down pocket linings and pocket top edges. Sew on sleeves, placing center of top edge of sleeve to shoulder seam. Join side and sleeve seams, reversing seam on lower half of cuffs. Turn back cuffs. Sew on buttons. Place belt at

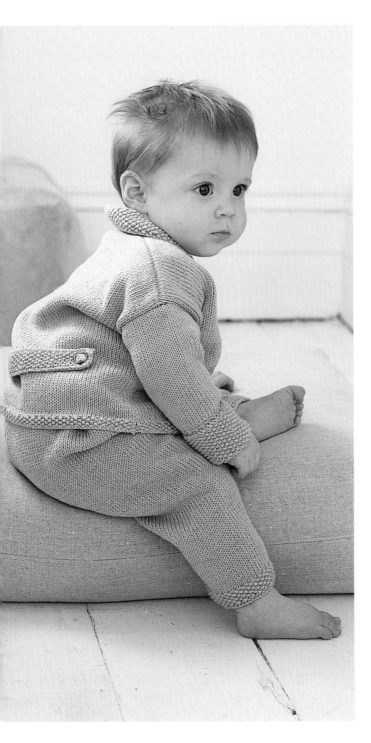

desired position on back and secure in place with buttons.

LEGGINGS
Left Leg
With US 2(2¾mm) needles cast on 69(83) sts.

Beg with a k row, work 1¼in/3cm in st st, ending with a p row.

K 3 rows.

Beg with a p row, cont in st st until work measures 7¾(9)in/20(23)cm from cast on edge, ending with a p row.

Shape inside leg

Dec one st at each end of next and every foll 3rd(4th) row until 49(59) sts rem.

Cont straight until work measures 4(6)in/10(15)cm from beg of leg shaping, ending with a p row.

Seed st row K1, * p1, k1; rep from * to end.

Rep this row 5 times more.

Bind off in seed st.

Right Leg
Work exactly as Left Leg.

Finish
Join center back and front seams. Join inside leg seams. Fold top edge over onto wrong side along ridge row to form a hem and slip stitch in place, leaving an opening in the seam. Thread elastic through hem, stitch ends together, then stitch seam opening closed.

garter stitch jacket and hat

This simple knit is worked all in one, and has neat, turned-back cuffs. Both hat and jacket are worked in garter stitch, which is the easiest stitch of all.

Measurements

Jacket:

To fit ages	3-6	6-9	9-12	mths
Actual measurements				
Chest	22	24	26	in
	56	61	66	cm
Length to shoulder				
	10¼	11	11¾	in
	26	28	30	cm
Sleeve length (with cuff turned back)				
	6¼	7	8	in
	6	18	20	cm

Hat:

To fit ages   3-6   6-12 mths

Materials

Jacket: 4(5:6) 50g/2oz balls of Debbie Bliss cashmerino aran. Pair of US 8(5mm) knitting needles. 4 buttons.
Hat: 1(2) 50g/2oz balls of Debbie Bliss cashmerino aran. Pair of US 8(5mm) knitting needles.

Gauge

18 sts and 36 rows to 4in/10cm square over garter st (k every row) using US 8(5mm) needles.

Abbreviations See page 7.

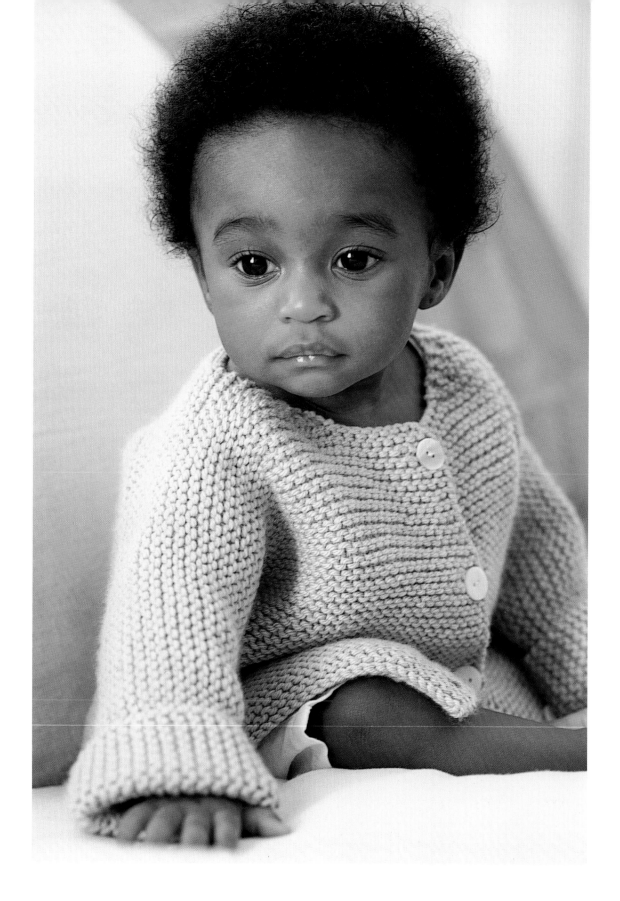

JACKET

Worked all in one piece.

With US 8(5mm) needles cast on 52(57:62) sts.

K 55(59:63) rows.

Shape sleeves

Cast on 6(7:8) sts at beg of next 6 rows and 18(20:22) sts at beg of foll 2 rows. 124(139:154) sts.

K 32(36:40) rows.

Divide for Fronts

Next row K51(58:65) sts, bind off next 22(23:24) sts, k to end.

Cont on last set of 51(58:65) sts for left front.

K 7(9:11) rows.

Shape neck

Inc one st at neck edge on next 6 rows.

Cast on 8 sts at beg of next row. 65(72:79) sts.

K 18(20:22) rows.

Shape sleeve

Bind off 18(20:22) sts at beg of next row and 6(7:8) sts at beg of 3 foll alt rows. 29(31:33) sts.

K 28(32:36) rows.

Make pocket opening

Next row K6(7:8), k next 17 sts and slip these sts onto a holder, k rem 6(7:8) sts.

Next row K6(7:8), cast on 17 sts, k rem 6(7:8) sts.

K 25 rows.

Bind off.

Right Front

With wrong side facing, join yarn to rem sts, k to end.

K 7(9:11) rows.

Shape neck

Inc one st at neck edge on next 6 rows.

Cast on 8 sts at beg of next row.

K 4 rows.

Buttonhole row K to last 4 sts, yf, k2tog, k2.

K11(13:15) rows.

Shape sleeve

Bind off 18(20:22) sts at beg of next row and 6(7:8) sts at beg of 3 foll alt rows. 29(31:33) sts.

K 3 rows.

Buttonhole row K to last 4 sts, yf, k2tog, k2.

K21(23:25) rows.

Buttonhole row K to last 4 sts, yf, k2tog, k2.

K3(5:7) rows.

Make pocket opening

Next row K6(7:8), k next 17 sts and slip these sts onto a holder, k rem 6(7:8) sts.

Next row K6(7:8), cast on 17 sts , k rem 6(7:8) sts.

K 16 rows.

Buttonhole row K to last 4 sts, yf, k2tog, k2.

K 8 rows. Bind off.

Pocket Linings (both alike)

With wrong side facing, slip sts from holder onto a US 8 (5mm) needle, join on yarn.

K 24 rows. Bind off.

Finish

Join side and sleeve seams, reversing seam on cuff for 2¼in/6cm. Sew down pocket linings. Sew on buttons. Turn back cuffs.

HAT

With US 8(5mm) needles cast on 64(71) sts.

Beg with a k row, work 8 rows in st st.

Cont in garter st until hat measures 5(6)in/13(15)cm from cast on edge.

Shape top

1st dec row K1, [k2tog, k5] 9(10) times. 55(61) sts.

K 3 rows.

2nd dec row K1, [k2tog, k4] 9(10) times. 46(51) sts.

K 3 rows.

Cont to dec in this way on next and foll 2 alt rows. 19(21) sts.

Next row K1, [k2tog] to end. 10(11) sts.

Break yarn, thread through rem sts, pull up and secure.

Join seam.

kimono and trousers

This relaxed, wrapover-style kimono has a tie belt and matching trousers. Worked in stockinette stitch with garter stitch borders, the set is a simple rather than an easy knit.

Measurements

Kimono: To fit ages

3-6	6-12	12-18	mths

Actual measurements

Chest

21¼	22¾	24½	in
54	58	62	cm

Length to shoulder

12½	13½	14¼	in
32	34	36	cm

Sleeve length

6¼	7	8	in
16	18	20	cm

Trousers: To fit ages

3-6	6-12	12-18	mths

Actual measurements

Width

20½	22	23½	in
52	56	60	cm

Length

9¾	11¾	14½	in
25	30	37	cm

Inside leg seam

3¼	4¼	5½	in
8	11	14	cm

Materials

Kimono:
3(3:4) 50g/2oz balls of Debbie Bliss wool/cotton in Main shade (M) and one 50g/2oz ball in Contrast shade (C). Pair each of US 2(3mm) and US 3 (3¼mm) knitting needles.

Trousers:
3(3:3) 50g/2oz balls of Debbie Bliss wool/cotton in Main shade (M) and one 50g/2oz ball in Contrast shade (C). Pair each of US 2(3mm) and US 3 (3¼mm) knitting needles.
Waist length of ½in1cm wide elastic.

Gauge

25 sts and 34 rows to 4in/10cm square over st st using US 3(3¼mm) needles.

Abbreviations See page 7.

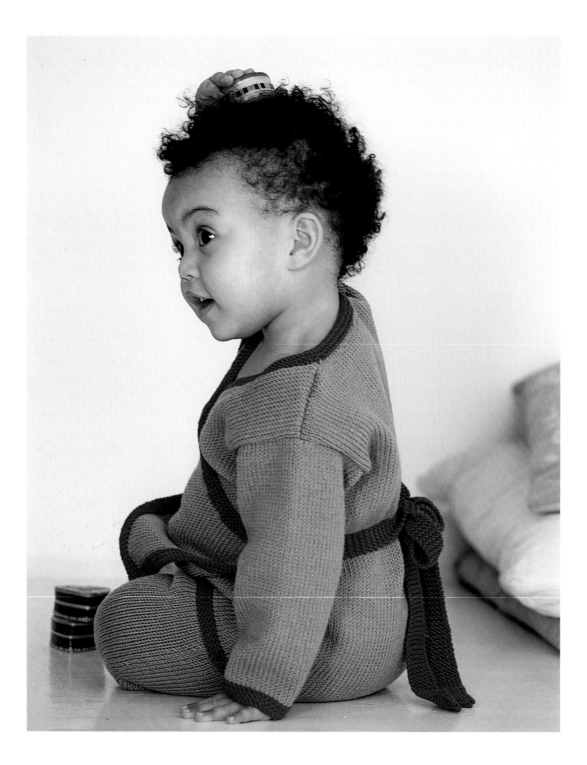

KIMONO

Back

With US 2 (3mm) needles and C, cast on 80(85:90) sts.

K 5 rows.

Change to US 3 (3¼mm) needles and M.

Beg with a k row, work 10(12:14) rows in st st.

Dec row K8, skpo, k to last 10 sts, k2tog, k8.

Cont in st st, work 9 rows.

Rep the last 10 rows 3 times more and the dec row once again. 70(75:80) sts.

Cont straight until back measures 8¼(8¾:9)in/21(22:23)cm from cast on edge, ending with a p row.

Shape armholes

Cast off 6 sts at beg of next 2 rows. 58(63:68) sts.

Cont straight until back measures 12½(13½:14¼)in/ 32(34:36)cm from cast on edge, ending with a p row.

Shape shoulders

Cast off 7(8:9) sts at beg of next 4 rows.

Leave rem 30(31:32) sts on a holder.

Left Front

With US 2 (3mm) needles and C, cast on 60(63:66) sts.

K 5 rows.

Change to US 3 (3¼mm) needles and M.

Beg with a k row, work 10(12:14) rows in st st.

Dec row (right side) K8, skpo, k to end.

Cont in st st, work 9 rows.

Rep the last 10 rows 3 times more and the dec row once again. 55(58:61) sts.

Work 2 rows, so ending with a k row.

Shape neck

Next row Bind off 7(8:9) sts, p to end. K 1 row.

Next row Bind off 5 sts, p to end. K 1 row.

Next row Bind off 4 sts, p to end.

Next row K to last 2 sts, k2tog.

Cont to dec one st at neck edge on every foll alt row until front measures same as Back to armhole shaping, ending with a p row.

Next row Bind off 6 sts, k to last 2 sts, k2tog.

Keeping armhole edge straight, cont to dec at neck edge on every alt row until 14(16:18) sts rem.

Cont straight until front measures same as Back to shoulder, ending at armhole edge.

Shape shoulder

Bind off 7(8:9) sts at beg of next row.

P 1 row.

Bind off rem 7(8:9) sts.

Right Front

With US 2 (3mm) needles and C, cast on 60(63:66) sts.

K 5 rows.

Change to US 3 (3¼mm) needles and M.

Beg with a k row, work 10(12:14) rows in st st.

Dec row K to last 10 sts, k2tog, k8.

Cont in st st, work 9 rows.

Rep the last 10 rows 3 times more and the dec row once again. 55(58:61) sts.

P 1 row.

Shape neck

Bind off 7(8:9) sts at beg of next row. P 1 row.

Bind off 5 sts at beg of next row. P 1 row.

Bind off 4 sts at beg of next row.

P 1 row.

Next row K2tog, k to end.

Cont to dec one st at neck edge on every foll alt row until front measures same as Back to armhole shaping, ending with a k row.

Next row Cast off 6 sts, p to end.

Keeping armhole edge straight, cont to dec at neck edge on every alt row until 14(16:18) sts rem.

Cont straight until front measures same as Back to shoulder, ending at armhole edge.

Shape shoulder

Bind off 7(8:9) sts at beg of next row.

K 1 row.

Bind off rem 7(8:9) sts.

Sleeves

With US 2 (3mm) needles and C, cast on 40(43:46) sts.
K 5 rows. Change to US 3 (3¼mm) needles and M.
Beg with a k row, work in st st, inc one st at each end of the 3rd and every foll 6th row until there are 54(59:66) sts.
Cont straight until sleeve measures 6¼(7:7¾)in/16(18:20)cm from cast on edge, mark each end of last row, then work a further 2cm/¾in, ending with a p row. Bind off.

Right Front Edging

With right side facing, US 2 (3mm) needles and C, pick up and k43(46:48) sts evenly along right front edge, from cast on edge to start of neck shaping. K 6 rows. Bind off.

Left Front Edging

With right side facing, US 2 (3mm) needles and C, pick up and k43(46:48) sts evenly along left front edge from start of neck shaping to cast on edge. K 6 rows. Bind off.

Neckband

Join shoulder seams.
With right side facing, US 2 (3mm) needles and C, pick up and k3 sts across row ends of right front band, 56(61:66) sts up right front neck, k across 30(31:32) sts at back neck, pick up and k56(61:66) sts down left front neck and 3 sts across row ends of left front band. 148(162:170) sts.
K 6 rows. Bind off.

Ties (make 2)

With US 2 (3mm) needles and C, cast on 6 sts.
Work in garter st until tie measures 17(18:19)in/43(46:48)cm from cast on edge. Bind off.

Finish

Sew on sleeves, sewing last ¾in/2cm above markers to sts bound off at underarm. Sew one tie to each end of neckband. Join side and sleeve seams, leaving an opening in right side seam, level with beg of neck shaping.

TROUSERS

Back and Front (both alike)

With US 2 (3mm) needles and M, cast on 66(72:78) sts.
Rib row * K1, p1; rep from * to end.
Rep the last row 9 times more.
Change to US 3 (3¼mm) needles. Beg with a k row, work in st st until work measures 6¾(7½:9)in/17(19:23)cm from cast on edge, ending with a p row.
Divide for legs
Next row K30(33:36) sts, turn and work on these sts for first leg.
P 1 row.
Dec one st at inside edge of next and 4(5:6) foll alt rows. 25(27:29) sts.
Cont straight until work measures 9½(11½:14¼)in/ 24(29:36)cm from cast on edge, ending with a p row.
Change to US 2 (3mm) needles and C. K 6 rows. Bind off.
With right side facing and M, rejoin yarn to rem sts, bind off 6 sts, k to end. Complete to match first leg.

To make up

Join side and inside leg seams. Join elastic into a ring.
Work a herringbone casing over wrong side of rib at waist, enclosing elastic.

pompon slippers

These slippers are knitted in garter stitch and are free of complicated shaping. For other decorative ideas, turn to page 124.

Measurements
To fit ages   6-12   12-18   months

Materials
One 50g/2oz ball of Debbie Bliss wool/cotton in Main shade (M) and small amount in Contrast shade (C). Pair of US 2(2¾mm) knitting needles.

Gauge
28 sts and 60 rows to 4in/10cm square over garter st (k every row) using US 2 (2¾mm) needles.

Abbreviations See page 7.

Note For safety reasons, make sure pompons are sewn on securely.

To make
With US 2 (2¾mm) needles and M, cast on 22(26) sts.
K 1 row.
Work in garter st and inc one st at each end of next and every foll alt row until there are 38(44) sts.
Dec one st at each end of next and every foll alt row until 22(26) sts rem.
Shape heel
Next row Cast on 8(9) sts, k these 8(9) sts, then k to end. 30(35) sts.
K 1 row.
Inc one st at end of next and 6(7) foll alt rows. 37(43) sts.
K 1 row.
Next row Bind off 20(22) sts, k to last st, inc in last st. 18(22) sts.
K 18(22) rows.
Next row K2tog, k to end.
Next row Cast on 20(22) sts, k these 20(22) sts, k to end. 37(43) sts.
Dec one st at beg of next and 6(7) foll alt rows. 30(35) sts.
K 1 row.
Bind off.

Finish
Join back heel seam. Join upper to sole all around, easing in fullness at toes. Turn through to right side. With C, make two small pompons and attach to top of slippers.

raglan sweater

Beautifully simple, this sweater has soft, rolling edges and fully fashioned detailing on the raglan shaping. The cashmere content of the yarn makes it soft against a baby's skin.

Measurements
To fit ages

| 0-3 | 3-6 | 6-9 | 9-12 | mths |

Actual measurements

Chest

| 19 | 20½ | 22 | 24 | in |
| 48 | 52 | 56 | 61 | cm |

Length to shoulder

| 8¾ | 9½ | 10¼ | 11 | in |
| 22 | 24 | 26 | 28 | cm |

Sleeve length

| 5½ | 6¼ | 7 | 8 | in |
| 14 | 16 | 18 | 20 | cm |

Materials
3(3:4:4) 50g/2oz balls of Debbie Bliss cashmerino aran.
Pair of US 8(5mm) knitting needles.

Gauge
18 sts and 24 rows to 4in/10cm square over st st using No 8(5mm) needles.

Abbreviations See page 7.

Back and Front (both alike)
With US 8(5mm) needles, cast on 45(49:53:57) sts.
Beg with a k row, work in st st until work measures 4¼(4¾:5:5½)in /11(12:13:14)cm from cast on edge, ending with a p row.

Shape raglan
Bind off 3 sts at beg of next 2 rows.
1st row K2, skpo, k to last 4 sts, k2tog, k2.
2nd row P to end.
Rep the last 2 rows until 19(21:23:25) sts rem, ending with a p row. Beg with a k row, work 2 rows st st.
Bind off.

Sleeves
With US 8(5mm) needles cast on 30(32:34:36) sts.
Beg with a k row, work 6 rows st st.
Inc row (right side) K3, m1, k to last 3 sts, m1, k3.
Work 3 rows st st.
Cont in st st and inc as before on next and every foll 4th row until there are 40(44:48:52) sts.
Cont straight until sleeve measures 5½(6¼:7:8)in/ 14(16:18:20)cm from cast on edge, ending with a p row.
Shape raglan
Bind off 3 sts at beg of next 2 rows.
1st row K2, skpo, k to last 4 sts, k2tog, k2.
2nd row P to end.
Rep the last 2 rows until 14(16:18:20) sts rem, ending with a p row. Beg with a k row, work 2 rows st st. Bind off.

Finish
Join raglan seams. Join side and sleeve seams.

two-color shoes

These ankle-strap baby shoes, worked in toning shades, can be teamed with the kimono and trousers on page 30.

Measurements
To fit ages

| 3-6 | 6-9 | 9-12 | mths |

Materials
One 50g/2oz ball of Debbie Bliss wool/cotton in Main shade (M) and small amount Contrast shade (C).
Pair of US 2(3mm) knitting needles.
2 buttons.

Gauge
26 sts and 56 rows to 4in/10cm square over garter st (k every row) using US 2(3mm) needles.

Abbreviations See page 7.

Right Shoe
With US 2(3mm) needles and C, cast on 35(39:45) sts.
K 1 row.
Change to M. Slip first 13(14:16) sts onto a holder, join on yarn to rem sts, k9(11:13) sts, leave rem 13(14:16) sts on a holder.
K 15(17:19) rows for instep. Break off yarn.
With right side facing, k across first 13(14:16) sts on holder, pick up and k12(13:14) sts along row ends of instep, k across 9(11:13) sts of instep, pick up and k12(13:14) sts along row ends of instep, k across 13(14:16) sts on holder. 59(65:73) sts.
K 7(9:13) rows.
Next row [K1, skpo, k24(27:31), k2tog] twice, k1. K 1 row.
Next row [K1, skpo, k22(25:29), k2tog] twice, k1. K 1 row.
Next row [K1, skpo, k20(23:27), k2tog] twice, k1. K 1 row.
Next row [K1, skpo, k18(21:25), k2 tog] twice, k1. K 1 row.
2nd and 3rd sizes only
Next row [K1, skpo, (19:23), k2tog] twice, k1. K 1 row.
3rd size only
Next row [K1, skpo, k(21), k2tog] twice, k1. K 1 row.
All sizes
Bind off.
Join sole and back seam.
With right side facing, US 2(3mm) needles and C, and beg and ending 6(7:8) sts to each side of back seam, pick up and k13(15:17) sts along heel edge. K 1 row. **
Next row (right side) Cast on 3 sts, k to end, turn and cast on 17(18:19) sts. K 1 row.
Buttonhole row K29(32:35), yf, k2tog, k2.
K 2 rows. Bind off. Sew on button.

Left Shoe
Work as given for Right Shoe to **.
Next row (right side) Cast on 17(18:19) sts, k to end, turn and cast on 3 sts. K 1 row.
Buttonhole row K2, k2tog, yf, k to end.
K 2 rows. Bind off. Sew on button.

classic cardigan

This stockinette stitch cardigan knits up quickly in an Aran-weight yarn. A cotton and silk mixture, the yarn lends the fabric of this classic style a slight hint of sheen.

Measurements

To fit ages

3-6	6-9	9-12	12-24	24-36 mths

Actual measurements

Chest

20½	22	23½	25½	27¼	in
52	56	60	65	69	cm

Length to shoulder

9½	10¼	11	12½	14¼	in
24	26	28	32	36	cm

Sleeve length

6	6¾	7½	8¾	9½	in
15	17	19	22	24	cm

Materials

6(6:7:8:9) 50g/2oz balls of Debbie Bliss cotton/silk aran.
Pair each of US 6(4mm) and US 7 (4½mm) knitting needles.
5(5:5:6:6) buttons

Gauge

18 sts and 24 rows to 4in/10cm square over st st using US 7(4½mm) needles.

Abbreviations See page 7.

Back and Fronts

Worked in one piece to armholes.

With US 6(4mm) needles cast on 92(100:108:116:124) sts.

1st row (right side) K3, * p2, k2; rep from * to last 5 sts, p2, k3.

2nd row P3, * k2, p2; rep from * to last 5 sts, k2, p3.

Rep these 2 rows 1(1:2:2:2) times more.

Change to US 7(4½mm) needles.

Beg with a k row, work in st st until work measures 4¾(5:5½:6¾:8)in/12(13:14:17:20)cm from cast on edge, ending with a p row.

Divide for Back and Fronts

Next row K21(23:25:27:29), leave these sts on a holder for right front, bind off 4 sts, k until there are 42(46:50:54:58) sts on needle, leave these sts on a holder for back, bind off 4 sts, k to end.

Left Front

Cont on last set of 21(23:25:27:29) sts only.

Dec one st at armhole edge on 2(3:4:4:5) foll alt rows. 19(20:21:23:24) sts.

Cont straight until work measures 7½(8¼:8¾:10¼:11½)in/ 19(21:22:26:29)cm from cast on edge, ending at front edge.

Shape neck

Next row P3(4:4:5:5) sts, place these sts on a holder, p to end.

Dec one st at neck edge on every row until 12(13:14:15:15) sts rem.

Cont straight until work measures 9½(10¼:11:12½:14¼)in/ 24(26:28:32:36)cm from cast on edge, ending at armhole edge. Bind off.

Back

With wrong side facing, rejoin yarn to next st, p42(46:50:54:58) sts.

Shape armholes

Dec one st at each end of next and 1(2:3:3:4) foll alt rows. 38(40:42:46:48) sts.

Cont straight until back measures same as Front to shoulder, ending with a wrong side row.

Shape shoulders

Bind off 12(13:14:15:15) sts at beg of next 2 rows.

Leave rem 14(14:14:16:18) sts on a holder.

Right Front

With wrong side facing, rejoin yarn to next st, p21(23:25:27:29) sts.

Dec one st at armhole edge on 2(3:4:4:5) foll alt rows. 19(20:21:23:24) sts.

Cont straight until work measures 7½(8¼:8¾:10¼:11½)in/ 19(21:22:26:29)cm from cast on edge, ending at front edge.

Shape neck

Next row (right side) K3(4:4:5:5) sts, place these sts on a holder, k to end.

Dec one st at neck edge on every row until 12(13:14:15:15) sts rem.

Cont straight until right front measures same as Left Front to shoulder, ending at armhole edge.

Bind off.

Sleeves

With US 6(4mm) needles cast on 30(30:34:34:38) sts.

1st row (right side) K2, * p2, k2; rep from * to end.

2nd row P2, * k2, p2; rep from * to end.

Rep the last 2 rows 1(1:1:2:2) times more.

Change to US 7(4½mm) needles.

Beg with a k row, work in st st, inc one st at each end of the 3rd and every foll 4th row until there are 44(48:52:56:60) sts.

Cont straight until sleeve measures 6(6¾:7½:8¾:9½)in/ 15(17:19:22:24)cm from cast on edge, ending with a p row.

Shape top

Bind off 3 sts at beg of next 2 rows.

Dec one st at each end of next and 1(2:3:3:4) foll alt rows. 34(36:38:42:44) sts.

Work 1 row. Bind off.

Neckband

Join shoulder seams.

With right side facing and US 6(4mm) needles, slip 3(4:4:5:5) sts from right front neck holder onto a needle, pick up and k12(13:15:15:16) sts up right front neck, k14(14:14:16:18) sts from back neck holder, pick up and k12(13:15:15:16) sts down left side of front neck, k3(4:4:5:5) sts from left front holder. 44(48:52:56:60) sts.

1st row (wrong side) P3, * k2, p2; rep from * to last 5 sts, k2, p3.

2nd row K3, * p2, k2; rep from * to last 5 sts, p2, k3.

3rd row P3, * k2, p2; rep from * to last 5 sts, k2, p3.

Bind off in rib.

Button Band

With right side facing and US 6(4mm) needles, pick up and k46(50:54:62:70) sts evenly along left front edge.

1st row (wrong side) P2, * k2, p2; rep from * to end.

2nd row K2, * p2, k2; rep from * to end.

3rd row P2, * k2, p2; rep from * to end. Bind off in rib.

Buttonhole Band

With right side facing and US 6(4mm) needles, pick up and k46(50:54:66:70) sts evenly along right front edge.

1st row (wrong side) P2, * k2, p2; rep from * to end.

2nd row Rib 2, [yrn, rib 2tog, rib 8(9:10:10:11)] 4(4:4:5:5) times, yrn, rib 2tog, rib 2(2:2:2:1).

3rd row Rib to end. Bind off in rib.

Finish

Sew sleeves into armholes. Join sleeve seams. Sew on buttons.

cozy

donkey jacket and shoes

With its warm lining and generous hood with ears, this is a jacket to snuggle into. The shoes are created with double fabric for extra warmth.

Measurements

Jacket:

To fit ages	6	12	12-18	mths

Actual measurements

Chest	22	24½	27½	in
	56	62	70	cm

Length to shoulder

	10¼	12	13¼	in
	26	30	34	cm

Sleeve length (with cuff turned back)

	6¼	7	8	in
	16	18	20	cm

Shoes: To fit 6-12 mths

Materials

Jacket: 5(6:7) 50g/2oz balls of Debbie Bliss cashmerino aran in each of Main shade (M) and Contrast shade (C). Pair each of US 7(4½mm) and US 8(5mm) long knitting needles. Two stitch holders. 3 buttons.

Shoes: One 50g/2oz ball of Debbie Bliss cashmerino aran in each of Main shade (M) and Contrast shade (C). Pair each of US 7 (4½mm) and US 8(5mm) knitting needles.

Gauges

18 sts and 24 rows to 4in/10cm square over st st using US 8(5mm) needles.
19 sts and 25 rows to 4in/10cm square over st st using US 7(4½mm) needles.

Abbreviations See page 7.

JACKET LINING

Back and Fronts

Worked in one piece to armholes.

With US 7(4½mm) needles and C, cast on 112 (124:140) sts.

Beg with a k row, work in st st.

Work 18(22:26) rows.

1st buttonhole row K to last 6 sts, bind off 2, k3.

2nd buttonhole row P4, cast on 2 sts, p to end.

Work a further 16(18:20) rows.

1st buttonhole row K to last 6 sts, bind off 2, k3.

2nd buttonhole row P4, cast on 2 sts, p to end.

Divide for Back and Fronts

Next row K29(32:36), leave these sts on a holder for left front, k next 54(60:68), leave these sts on a holder for back, k to end for right front.

Right Front

Work a further 15(17:19) rows.

1st buttonhole row K to last 6 sts, bind off 2, k3.

2nd buttonhole row P4, cast on 2 sts, p to end.

Work a further 10(12:14) rows.

Shape shoulder

Next row Bind off 14(16:18) sts, k to end.

Next row P to end and leave these 15(16:18) sts on a spare needle.

Back

With wrong side facing, rejoin yarn to next st.

Work a further 27(31:35) rows.

Shape shoulders

Bind off 14(16:18) sts at beg of next 2 rows.

Bind off rem 26(28:32) sts.

Left Front

With wrong side facing, rejoin yarn to next st.

Work a further 28(32:36) rows.

Shape shoulder

Next row Bind off 14(16:18) sts, p to end and leave these 15(16:18) sts on needle.

Do not break off yarn.

Hood

Join shoulder seams.

Next row With US 7(4½mm) needles and C, k across 15(16:18) sts of left front, cast on 38(42:48) sts, k across 15(16:18) sts of right front. 68(74:84) sts.

Beg with a p row, work a further 51(53:55) rows.

Shape top

Next row K34(37:42) sts, turn and work on these sts for first side.

Bind off 8(9:10) sts at beg of next and two foll alt rows.

Bind off rem 10(10:12) sts.

With right side facing, rejoin yarn to rem sts.

Bind off 8(9:10) sts at beg of next and two foll alt rows.

Bind off rem 10(10:12) sts.

Sleeves

With US 8(5mm) needles and C, cast on 28(32:36) sts.

Beg with a k row, work in st st.

Work 10 rows.

Change to US 7(4½mm) needles. Work 10 rows.

Cont in st st, inc one st at each end of the next and every foll 4th row until there are 42(48:54) sts.

Work 5 rows.

Bind off.

JACKET MAIN PART
Back and Fronts

Worked in one piece to armholes.

With US 8(5mm) needles and M, cast on 112(124:140) sts.

Beg with a k row, cont in st st.

Work 16(18:20) rows.

Pocket openings

Next row K9(10:11), bind off 15(17:19) sts, k next 63(69:79) sts, bind off 15(17:19) sts, k to end.

Next row K9(10:11), cast on 15(17:19) sts, k64(70:80) sts, cast on 15(17:19) sts, k9(10:11).

Work 0(2:4) rows.

1st buttonhole row K4, bind off 2 sts, k to end.

2nd buttonhole row P to last 4 sts, cast on 2 sts, p4.

Work a further 16(18:20) rows.

1st buttonhole row K4, bind off 2 sts, k to end.

2nd buttonhole row P to last 4 sts, cast on 2 sts, p4.

Divide for Back and Fronts

Next row K29(32:36), leave these sts on a holder for right front, k next 54(60:68), leave these sts on a holder for back, k to end for left front.

Left Front

Work a further 27(31:35) rows.

Shape shoulder

Next row Bind off 14(16:18) sts, k to end.

P 1 row.

Leave rem 15(16:18) sts on a spare needle.

Back

With wrong side facing, rejoin yarn to next st.

Work a further 27(31:35) rows.

Shape shoulders

Bind off 14(16:18) sts at beg of next 2 rows.

Bind off rem 26(28:32) sts.

Right Front

With wrong side facing, rejoin yarn to next st.

Work a further 15(17:19) rows.

1st buttonhole row K4, bind off 2 sts, k to end.

2nd buttonhole row P to last 4 sts, cast on 2 sts, p4.

Work a further 11(13:15) rows.

Shape shoulder

Next row Bind off 14(16:18) sts, p to end and leave these 15(16:18) sts on needle.

Do not break off yarn.

Hood

Join shoulder seams.

Next row With US 8(5mm) needles and M, k across 15(16:18) sts of right front, cast on 38(42:48) sts, k across 15(16:18) sts of left front. 68(74:84) sts.

Beg with a p row, work a further 51(53:55) rows.

Shape top

Next row K34(37:42) sts, turn and work on these sts for first side.

Bind off 8(9:10) sts at beg of next and two foll alt rows.

Bind off rem 10(10:12) sts.

Rejoin yarn to rem sts.

Bind off 8(9:10) sts at beg of next and two foll alt rows.

Bind off rem 10(10:12) sts.

Sleeves

With US 7(4½mm) needles and M, cast on 28(32:36) sts.

Beg with a k row, work in st st.

Work 20 rows.

Change to US 8(5mm) needles.

Cont in st st, inc one st at each end of the next and every foll 4th row until there are 42(48:54) sts.

Work 5 rows. Bind off.

Ears (make 2)

With US 8(5mm) needles and M, cast on 6 sts.

Beg with a k row, work 2 rows st st.

Next row K3, m1, k3.

Work 1 row.

Next row K3, m1, k1, m1, k3.

Work 1 row.

Next row K4, m1, k1, m1, k4.

Work 1 row.

Next row K5, m1, k1, m1, k5.

Work 1 row.

Next row K6, m1, k1, m1, k6.

Work 1 row.

Next row K7, m1, k1, m1, k7. 17 sts.

Work 7 rows.

Next row K1, skpo, k11, k2tog, k1.

Work 3 rows.
Next row K1, skpo, k9, k2tog, k1.
Work 3 rows.
Next row K1, skpo, k7, k2tog, k1.
Work 3 rows.
Next row K1, skpo, k5, k2tog, k1.
Work 3 rows.
Next row K1, skpo, k3, k2tog, k1.
Work 3 rows.
Next row K1, skpo, k1, k2tog, k1.
Work 3 rows.
Next row K1, s1 1, k2tog, psso, k1.
Bind off rem 3 sts.

Ear Linings (make 2)
With US 7(4½mm) needles and C, work as given for Ears.

Finish
Join top seam of hood, then join cast on edge of hood to sts bound off at back neck, easing to fit. Join sleeve seams. Sew sleeves into armholes. Using mattress st and matching row for row and stitch for stitch, with wrong side of lining to wrong side of coat, join lining to coat, around all edges. Join lining and coat buttonhole edges together. Sew on buttons. Sew ear linings to ears in pairs and sew to top of hood. Sew cast on edge of pocket opening to lining.
Make a pocket below opening, by sewing main part and lining together.

SHOES
Main Part (make 2)
With US 8(5mm) needles and M, cast on 3 sts.
Next row P to end.
Next row K1, m1, k1, m1, k1.
Next row P to end.
Next row K1, m1, k3, m1, k1.
Next row P to end.
Next row K1, m1, k5, m1, k1.

Cont in this way to inc 2 sts on every alt row until there are 25 sts.
Next row P to end.
Next row K1, skpo, k to last 3 sts, k2tog, k1.
Rep the last 2 rows until 5 sts rem.
Next row P to end.
Next row K1, sl 1, k2tog, psso, k1.
Next row P to end. Bind off.

Linings (make 2)
With US 7(4½mm) needles and C, work as given for Main Part.

Heel (make 2)
With US 8(5mm) needles and M, cast on 3 sts.
Next row P to end.
Next row K1, m1, k1, m1, k1.
Next row P to end.
Next row K1, m1, k3, m1, k1.
Next row P to end.
Next row K1, m1, k5, m1, k1.
Cont in this way to inc 2 sts on every alt row until there are 25 sts.
Next row P to end.
Change to US 7(4½mm) needles and C.
Next row K1, skpo, k to last 3 sts, k2tog, k1.
Rep the last 2 rows until 5 sts rem.
Next row P to end.
Next row K1, sl 1, k2tog, psso, k1.
Next row P to end. Bind off.

Finish
With wrong sides together, join one lining piece to each main piece. Fold three corners into center to form an open envelope and sew in place. Fold heel section in half across center and sew outside edges together, place joined edges of triangle to edges of open envelope, matching points. Sew in place.

hooded blanket

Worked in cashmerino aran, this seed stitch hooded blanket is ideal for wrapping up baby after the bath, or when a summer's day turns chillier.

Measurements
Approximately 26 x 26in/66 x 66cm.

Materials
Nine 50g/2oz balls of Debbie Bliss cashmerino aran.
Pair each of US 7(4½mm) and US 8 (5mm) knitting needles.

Gauge
20 sts and 36 rows to 4in/10cm square over seed st using US 8 (5mm) needles.

Abbreviations See page 7.

Blanket
With US 7(4½mm) needles cast on 133 sts.
K 5 rows.
Change to US 8(5mm) needles.
Next row K3, * p1, k1; rep from * to last 4 sts, p1, k3.
Repeat this row until blanket measures 25½in/65cm from cast on edge.
Change to US 7(4½mm) needles. K 4 rows. Bind off.

Hood
With US 8(5mm) needles cast on 2 sts.
1st row K2.
2nd row K1, m1, k1.
3rd row K to end.
4th row K1, m1, k1, m1, k1.
5th row K to end.
6th row K2, m1, k1, m1, k2.
7th row K to end.
8th row K3, m1, k1, m1, k3.
9th row K3, p1, k1, p1, k3.
10th row K3, m1, p1, k1, p1, m1, k3.
11th row K4, p1, k1, p1, k4.
12th row K3, m1, [k1, p1] twice, k1, m1, k3.
13th row K3, [p1, k1] 3 times, p1, k3.
Cont in this way, inc one st inside the 3 st border, at each end of every alt row until there are 75 sts.
Change to US 7(4½mm) needles. K 4 rows. Bind off.

Finish
Sew hood to corner of blanket.

cable and rib sweater with hood

This textured sweater has a shawl collar that turns into a hood. It is knitted in a crisp, double knitting cotton to make it the ideal all-seasons top.

Measurements

To fit ages

1	2	3	4	years

Actual measurements

Chest

24¾	28	32	35½	in
63	71	81	90	cm

Length to shoulder

12½	14½	16½	17¾	in
32	37	42	45	cm

Sleeve length (with cuff turned back)

7¾	8¾	9½	11	in
20	22	24	28	cm

Materials

10(11:12:13) 50g/2oz balls of Debbie Bliss cotton double knitting.
Pair each of US 5(3¾mm) and US 6 (4mm) knitting needles.
Cable needle.

Gauges

20 sts and 28 rows to 4in/10cm square over st st using US 6(4mm) needles.
24 sts and 32 rows to 4in/10cm square over patt using US 6(4mm) needles.

Abbreviations

C4B = cable 4 back, slip next 2 sts onto cable needle and leave at back of work, k2, then k2 from cable needle. See also page 7.

Back

With US 5(3¾mm) needles cast on 78(88:98:108) sts.

1st and 3rd sizes only

1st row P2, * k4, p2, k2, p2; rep from * to last 6 sts, k4, p2.
2nd row K2, * p4, k2, p2, k2; rep from * to last 6 sts, p4, k2.
3rd row P2, * C4B, p2, k2, p2; rep from * to last 6 sts, C4B, p2.
4th row K2, * p4, k2, p2, k2; rep from * to last 6 sts, p4, k2.
These 4 rows form the patt.

2nd and 4th sizes only

1st row P3, * k2, p2, k4, p2; rep from * to last 5 sts, k2, p3.
2nd row K3, * p2, k2, p4, k2; rep from * to last 5 sts, p2, k3.
3rd row P3, * k2, p2, C4B, p2; rep from * to last 5 sts, k2, p3.
4th row K3, * p2, k2, p4, k2; rep from * to last 5 sts, p2, k3.
These 4 rows form the patt.

All sizes

Work a further 8 rows.
Change to US 6(4mm) needles.
Cont in patt until back measures 12½(14½:16½:17¾)in/ 32(37:42:45)cm from cast on edge, ending with a wrong side row.

Shape shoulders

Bind off 21(24:28:33) sts at beg of next 2 rows.
Bind off rem 36(40:42:42) sts.

Front

Work as given for Back until front measures 7¾(9:10¼:11)in/ 20(23:26:28)cm from cast on edge, ending with a wrong side row.

Shape neck

Next row Patt 31(34:38:43) sts, turn and work on these sts

for first side of neck.

Cont straight until front measures the same as Back to shoulder, ending at side edge.

Next row Bind off 21(24:28:33) sts, patt to end.

Leave rem 10 sts on a holder.

With right side facing, bind off center 16(20:24:22) sts, patt to end.

Complete to match first side.

Sleeves

With US 6(4mm) needles cast on 42(42:50:50) sts.

1st rib row K2, * p2, k2; rep from * to end.

2nd rib row P2, * k2, p2; rep from * to end.

Rep the last 2 rows for 1½(1½:2:2)in/4(4:5:5)cm.

Change to US 5(3¾mm) needles.

Work 1½(1½:2:2)in/4(4:5:5)cm in rib, ending with a 1st rib row.

Inc row P2, * k2, m1, p2, m1, k2, p2; rep from * to end. 52(52:62:62) sts.

Change to US 6(4mm) needles.

1st row K2, * p2, k4, p2, k2; rep from * to end.

2nd row P2, * k2, p4, k2, p2; rep from * to end.

3rd row K2, * p2, C4B, p2, k2; rep from * to end.

4th row P2, * k2, p4, k2, p2; rep from * to end.

These 4 rows form the patt.

Cont in patt, at the same time, inc one st at each end of the next and every foll 4th row until there are 76(80:92:96) sts, taking inc sts into patt.

Cont straight until sleeve measures 9½(10¼:11½:13)in/ 24(26:29:33)cm from cast on edge, ending with a wrong side row.

Bind off.

Hood

Join shoulder seams.

With right side facing and using US 6(4mm) needles, k across 10 sts on right front neck holder, cast on 52(56:60:64) sts, k across 10 sts on left front neck holder. 72(76:80:84) sts.

Next row P3, * k2, p2; rep from * to last 5 sts, k2, p3.

Next row K3, * p2, k2; rep from * to last 5 sts, p2, k3.

Rep the last 2 rows until hood measures 7½(7¾:8¼:8¾)in/ 19(20:21:22)cm, ending with a wrong side row.

Shape top

Next row Patt 36(38:40:42) sts, turn and work on these sts.

Bind off 6 sts at beg of next and 4 foll alt rows.

Work 1 row.

Bind off rem 6(8:10:12) sts.

With right side facing, rejoin yarn to rem sts, bind off 6, patt to end.

Complete to match first side.

Right Front Border

With right side facing and US 5(3¾mm) needles, pick up and k74(82:90:98) sts along right front edge and right side of hood.

1st row P2, * k2, p2; rep from * to end.

2nd row K2, * p2, k2; rep from * to end.

Rep the last 2 rows for 2¾(3¼:3½:4)in/7(8:9:10)cm, ending with a 1st row.

Bind off in rib.

Left Front Border

With right side facing and US 5(3¾mm) needles, pick up and k74(82:90:98) sts along left side of hood and left front edge.

Work 2¾(3¼:3½:4)in/7(8:9:10)cm in rib as given for right front border.

Bind off.

Finish

With right sides together, fold hood in half and join shaped edge and borders, reversing seam on last 2(2¼:2¾:3¼)in/ 5(6:7:8)cm of border. Sew cast on edge of hood to bound off sts of back neck. Lap right front border over left front border and sew to bound off sts at center front. Sew on sleeves. Join side and sleeve seams.

circular yoked sweater

This enveloping, generous sweater has a colorful, patterned yoke. All the ribbed edges have a contrasting color stripe to emphasize the shades in the Fair Isle pattern.

Measurements

To fit ages 2-3, 3-4, 4-5 years

Actual measurements

	2-3	3-4	4-5	
Chest	28	31½	35	in
	71	80	89	cm
Length	15¾	18	20	in
	40	46	51	cm

Sleeve length (with cuff turned back)

	8¾	10	11	in
	22	25	28	cm

Materials

6(6:8) 50g/2oz balls of Debbie Bliss merino aran in Main shade (M) Gray and one ball each in Khaki, Aqua, Red, Fuchsia and Cream.
Pair each of US 6(4mm) and US 8 (5mm) needles.
Long circular US 8(5mm) and US 6 (4mm) needles.

Gauge

18 sts and 24 rows to 4in/10cm square over st st using US 8(5mm) needles.

Abbreviations

p2sso = pass 2 slipped sts over.
See also page 7.

Note Read charts from right to left on **every** row. When working Fair Isle pattern, strand yarn not in use loosely across wrong side to keep fabric elastic.

Back and Front (both alike)

With US 6(4mm) needles and Red, cast on 66(74:82) sts.
1st row K2, * p2, k2; rep from * to end.
2nd row P2, * k2, p2; rep from * to end.
Rep the last 2 rows once more.
Change to M.
Work a further 4(4:6) rows in rib.
Change to US 8(5mm) needles.
Beg with a k row, work in st st until back measures 8¼(9¾:11)in/21(25:28)cm from cast on edge, ending with a p row.

Shape armholes

Bind off 4(5:6) sts at beg of next 2 rows. 58(64:70) sts.

Yoke shaping

Next row K14(17:20) sts, turn and work on these sts.
Next row Work 2tog, p to end.
Next row Work 2tog, k to last 2 sts, work 2tog.
Rep the last 2 rows 3(4:5) times more. 2 sts.
Work 2tog and fasten off.
With right side facing, slip center 30 sts onto a holder, join on yarn to rem sts, k to end.
Next row P to last 2 sts, work 2tog.
Next row Work 2tog, k to last 2 sts, work 2tog.
Rep the last 2 rows 3(4:5) times more. 2 sts.
Work 2tog and fasten off.

Sleeves

With US 6(4mm) needles and Aqua, cast on 38(42:46) sts.
1st row K2, * p2, k2; rep from * to end.
2nd row P2, * k2, p2; rep from * to end.
Rep the last 2 rows once more.

Change to M.

Work a further 10(12:14) rows in rib, inc 4 sts evenly across last row. 42(46:50) sts.

Change to US 8(5mm) needles.

Work in st st, inc one st at each end of the 5th and every foll 4th row until there are 62(70:78) sts.

Cont straight until sleeve measures 9¾(11½:13)in/ 25(29:33)cm from cast on edge, ending with a p row.

Shape sleeve top

Bind off 4(5:6) sts at beg of next 2 rows. 54(60:66) sts.

Next row Work 2tog, k to last 2 sts, work 2tog.

Next row P to end.

Rep the last 2 rows 3(4:5) times more.

Leave rem 46(50:54) sts on a spare needle.

Yoke

Join the 4 short raglan seams.

With right side facing, US 8(5mm) circular needle and M, k across 46(50:54) sts from top of left sleeve, pick up and k7(8:9) sts down left side of front neck, k across 30 sts from center front, pick up and k7(8:9) sts up right side of front neck, k across 46(50:54) sts from top of right sleeve, pick up and k7(8:9) sts down right side of back neck, k across 30 sts from center back, pick up and k7(8:9) sts up left side of back neck. 180(192:204) sts.

Now work in pattern as follows:

1st round Work across 1st row of Chart 1 to end of round.

2nd round Work across 2nd row of Chart 1 to end of round.

3rd round Using Cream, k to end.

4th round Work across 1st row of Chart 2 to end of round.

5th to 16th rounds Work in patt from Chart 2.

17th round Using Cream, k to end.

18th round Using Cream, k2, * k2tog, k4; rep from * to last 4 sts, k2tog, k2. 150(160:170) sts.

19th round Work across 1st row of Chart 3 to end of round.

20th round Work across 2nd row of Chart 3 to end of round.

21st round Using Cream, k to end.

22nd round Using Cream, k to end.

23rd round Work across 1st row of Chart 4 to end of round.

24th and 25th rounds Work in patt from Chart 4.

26th round Using Cream, * k2, sl 2tog, k1, p2sso; rep from * to end. 90(96:102) sts.

Change to M.

26th round K to end, decreasing 2(0:2) sts. 88(96:100) sts.

Change to US 6(4mm) circular needle.

Next round * K2, p2; rep from * to end.

Rep the last round 13 times more.

Next row Slip first 33(36:37) sts onto needle, join in Khaki, rib 44(48:50), join in Fuchsia, rib 44(48:50), turn.

Work backwards and forwards in rows, twisting yarns at color change to avoid holes.

Work 3 rows in rib with colors as set.

Bind off in rib.

Finish

Join side and sleeve seams, reversing last 1¼(1½:2)in/ 3(4:5)cm seam of cuff.

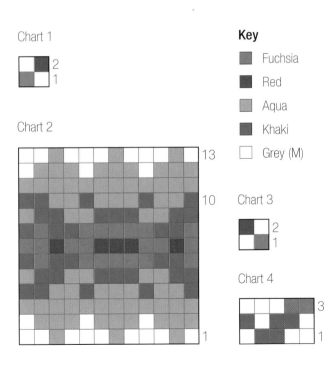

Chart 1

Chart 2

Key

- Fuchsia
- Red
- Aqua
- Khaki
- Grey (M)

Chart 3

Chart 4

zipped jacket with contrasting edges and hat

With its zipped front opening, pockets and contrasting color borders, this is a sporty jacket for an active child. For wintry days there is a cosy, ribbed hat.

Measurements

Jacket:

To fit ages	1	2	3	years
Actual measurements				
Chest	27¼	29½	31½	in
	69	75	80	cm
Length to shoulder				
	13½	15	16½	in
	34	38	42	cm
Sleeve length				
	7	8¾	9¾	in
	18	22	25	cm

Hat: To fit 1-2 2-3 years

Materials

Jacket: 6(7:8) 50g/2oz balls of Debbie Bliss merino aran in Main shade (M) and one ball in Contrast shade (C). Pair each of US 7 (4½mm) and US 8(5mm) knitting needles. 14(16:18)in/35(40:45)cm open-ended zip.

Hat: 2(2) 50g/2oz balls of Debbie Bliss merino aran in Main shade (M) and one ball in Contrast shade (C). Pair each of No 7 (4½mm) and No 8(5mm) knitting needles.

Gauge

18 sts and 24 rows to 4in/10cm square over st st using US 8(5mm) needles.

Abbreviations See page 7.

JACKET

Back

With US 7(4½mm) needles and M, cast on 62(68:72) sts.

K 3 rows.

Change to US 8(5mm) needles.

Beg with a k row, work in st st until back measures 12¼(13¾:15¼)in/31(35:39)cm from cast on edge, ending with a p row.

Shape back neck

Next row K24(26:28) sts, turn and work on these sts for first side of back neck.

Dec one st at neck edge of the next 4 rows.

Work 3 rows straight.

Shape shoulder

Bind off 10(11:12) sts at beg of next row.

Work 1 row.

Bind off rem 10(11:12) sts.

With right side facing, slip center 14(16:16) sts onto a holder, join on yarn, k to end.

Dec one st at neck edge of the next 4 rows.

Work 4 rows straight.

Shape shoulder

Bind off 10(11:12) sts at beg of next row.

Work 1 row. Bind off rem 10(11:12) sts.

Pocket Linings (make 2)

With US 8(5mm) needles and M, cast on 17(19:21) sts.

Beg with a k row, work in st st for 2(2½:2¾)in/5(6:7)cm, ending with a p row. Leave sts on a spare needle.

Left Front

With US 7(4½mm) needles and M, cast on 32(34:36) sts.
K 3 rows.

Change to US 8(5mm) needles.

Beg with a k row, work in st st until left front measures 2½(2¾:3)in/6(7:8)cm from cast on edge, ending with a k row.

Shape pocket top

Next row P24(26:28) sts, turn and work on these sts only.

Bind off 4 sts at beg of next row.

Dec one st at shaped edge of every row until 7 sts rem, ending with a wrong side row.

Leave these sts on a holder.

Place pocket

With wrong side facing, rejoin yarn, p rem 8 sts.

Next row K8, then k across sts of pocket lining. 25(27:29) sts.

Beg with a p row, work 13(15:17) rows in st st.

Next row K these sts, then k7 sts from holder. 32(34:36) sts.

Work straight until front measures 11½(13:14½)in/ 29(33:37)cm from cast on edge, ending with a k row.

Shape neck

Next row P8, slip these 8 sts onto a holder, p to end.

Dec one st at neck edge on every foll alt row until 20(22:24) sts rem.

Work straight until front measures same as Back to shoulder, ending at side edge.

Shape shoulder

Bind off 10(11:12) sts at beg of next row.

Work 1 row.

Bind off rem 10(11:12) sts.

Right Front

With US 7(4½mm) needles cast on 32(34:36) sts. K3 rows.
Change to US 8(5mm) needles.

Beg with a k row, work in st st until right front measures 2½(2¾:3)in/6(7:8)cm from cast on edge, ending with a p row.

Shape pocket top

Next row K24(26:28) sts, turn and work on these sts.

Bind off 4 sts at beg of next row.

Dec one st at shaped edge of every row until 7 sts rem, ending with a right side row.

Work 1 row. Leave these sts on a holder.

Place pocket

Next row K across sts of pocket lining, then k8 sts at side edge. 25(27:29) sts.

Beg with a p row, work 14(16:18) rows in st st, ending with a k row.

Next row P these sts, then p8 sts from holder. 32(34:36) sts.

Work straight until front measures 11½(13:14½)in/ 29(33:37)cm from cast on edge, ending with a p row.

Shape neck

Next row K8, slip these 8 sts onto a holder, k to end.

Dec one st at neck edge on every foll alt row until 20(22:24) sts rem.

Work straight until front measures same as Back to shoulder, ending at side edge.

Shape shoulder

Bind off 10(11:12) sts at beg of next row.

Work 1 row. Bind off rem 10(11:12) sts.

Sleeves

With US 7(4½mm) needles and C, cast on 30(34:38) sts.

1st rib row K2, * p2, k2; rep from * to end.

2nd rib row P2, * k2, p2; rep from * to end.

Change to M.

Rep the last 2 rows 3(4:4) times more, inc 8 sts evenly across last row. 38(42:46) sts.

Change to US 8(5mm) needles.

Beg with a k row, work in st st, inc one st at each end of the 3rd and every foll 4th row until there are 50(56:62) sts.

Cont straight until sleeve measures 7(8¾:9¾)in/18(22:25)cm from cast on edge, ending with a p row. Bind off.

Pocket Edgings

With right side facing, US 7(4½mm) needles and C, pick up and k17(19:21) sts, evenly along pocket opening edge.

K 3 rows. Bind off.

Collar

Join shoulder seams.

With US 7(4½mm) needles and M, slip 8 sts from holder onto needle, pick up and k15(16:17) sts up right front neck, 6 sts down right back neck, k14(16:18) sts from back neck holder, pick up and k6 sts up left back neck, 15(16:17) sts down left front neck, then k8 from holder. 72(76:80) sts.

Next row P3, * k2, p2; rep from * to last 5 sts, k2, p3.

Next row K3, * p2, k2; rep from * to last 5 sts, p2, k3.

Work a further 2(2½:3)in/5(6:7)cm in rib patt, ending with a right side row.

Change to C.

Work a further 3 rows. Bind off in rib.

Front Edgings

With right side facing, US 7(4½mm) needles and C, pick up and k66(76:86) sts along right front and collar edge.

K 3 rows. Bind off.

Rep for left front edging.

Finish

With center of sleeve edge to shoulder seam, sew on sleeves. Join side and sleeve seams. Sew in zip. Sew down pocket linings and tops.

HAT

With US 8(5mm) needles and C, cast on 86(98) sts.

1st rib row K2, * p2, k2; rep from * to end.

2nd rib row P2, * k2, p2; rep from * to end.

These 2 rows set the rib.

Rep 1st rib row. Change to M.

Cont in rib until work measures 1½in/4cm, ending with a 1st rib row.

Change to US 7(4½mm) needles.

Work in rib for a further 1½in/4cm.

Change to US 8(5mm) needles and cont in rib until hat measures 7(8)in/18(20)cm from cast on edge, ending with a 2nd rib row.

Shape top

1st row K2, * p2tog, k2; rep from * to end.

2nd row P2, * k1, p2; rep from * to end.

3rd row K2, * p1, k2; rep from * to end.

4th row P2, * k1, p2; rep from * to end.

5th row K2tog, * p1, k2tog; rep from * to end.

6th row P1, * k1, p1; rep from * to end.

7th row K1, * p3tog, k1; rep from * to last 2(0) sts, p1(0), k1(0).

8th row P1, * p2tog; rep from * to end.

Break yarn, thread end through rem 12(13) sts, pull up and secure.

Join seam, reversing seam on last 1½in/4cm.

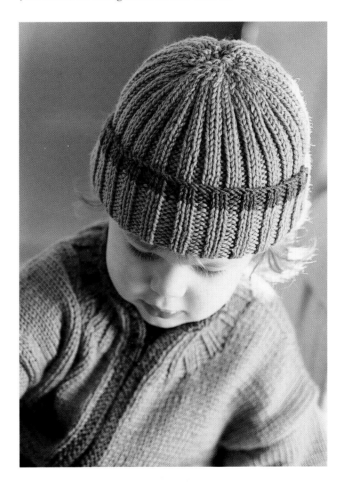

cable and seed stitch jacket

Knitted with a soft merino wool, this warm, cozy cabled jacket has seed stitch detailing on the pockets, yoke, and collar.

Measurements

To fit ages

6-12	12-18	18-24	mths

Actual measurements

Chest

24½	27½	31½	in
62	70	80	cm

Length

11¾	13	14¼	in
30	33	36	cm

Sleeve seam

6¼	7	9	in
16	18	23	cm

Materials

6(6:7) 50g/2oz balls of Debbie Bliss merino aran.
Pair of US 8(5mm) knitting needles.
7 buttons.

Gauge

18 sts and 24 rows to 4in/10cm square over st st using US 8(5mm) needles.

Abbreviations

C4F = cable 4 front, slip next 2 sts onto a cable needle and hold at the front of work, k2, then k2 from cable needle.
See also page 7.

Back

With US 8(5mm) needles cast on 72(80:88) sts.

1st row (right side) K1, [p1, k1] 3 times, * p1, k4, [p1, k1] 4(5:6) times; rep from * 3 times more, p1, k4, [p1, k1] 4 times.

2nd row [K1, p1] 3 times, * k2, p4, k1, [k1, p1] 3(4:5) times; rep from * 3 times more, k2, p4, k2, [p1, k1] 3 times.

3rd row K1, [p1, k1] 3 times, * p1, C4F, [p1, k1] 4(5:6) times; rep from * 3 times more, p1, k4, [p1, k1] 4 times.

4th row As 2nd row.

5th row As 1st row.

6th row [K1, p1] twice, p3, * k1, p4, k1, p7(9:11); rep from * 3 times more, k1, p4, k1, p3, [p1, k1] twice.

7th row [K1, p1] twice, k3, * p1, C4F, p1, k7(9:11); rep from * 3 times more, p1, C4F, p1, k3, [p1, k1] twice.

8th row As 6th row.

9th row [K1, p1] twice, k3, * p1, k4, p1, k7(9:11); rep from * 3 more times, p1, k4, p1, k3, [p1, k1] twice.

10th to 13th rows Rep 6th to 9th rows once more.

14th row P7, * k1, p4, k1, p7(9:11); rep from * 3 times more, k1, p4, k1, p7.

15th row K7, * p1, C4F, p1, k7(9:11); rep from * 3 times more, p1, C4F, p1, k7.

16th row As 14th row.

17th row K7, * p1, k4, p1, k7(9:11); rep from * 3 times more, p1, k4, p1, k7.

Rep the last 4 rows until back measures 6¼(7:7½)in/ 16(17.5:19)cm from cast on edge, ending with a wrong side row.

Work straight in cable and seed st patt as given for 1st to 4th patt rows, until back measures 11¾(13:14½)in/ 30(33:36)cm from cast on edge, ending with a wrong side row.

Shape shoulders

Working 2sts tog over each cable, bind off 21(23:25) sts at beg of next 2 rows.

Bind off rem 30(34:38) sts.

Pocket Linings (make 2)

With US 8(5mm) needles cast on 16(18:20) sts.
Beg with a k row, work 16(18:20) rows in st st.
Leave sts on a holder.

Left Front

With US 8(5mm) needles cast on 37(41:45) sts.
1st row (right side) K1, [p1, k1] 3 times, p1, k4, [p1, k1] 4(5:6) times, p1, k4, [p1, k1] 6(7:8) times.
2nd row [K1, p1] 5(6:7) times, k2, p4, k1, [k1, p1] 3(4:5) times, k2, p4, k1, [k1, p1] 3 times, k1.
3rd row * K1, [p1, k1] 3 times, p1, C4F, [p1, k1] 4(5:6) times, p1, C4F, [p1, k1] 6(7:8) times.
4th row As 2nd row.
5th row As 1st row.
6th row [K1, p1] twice, * p7(9:11), k1, p4, k1; rep from * once more, p3, [p1, k1] twice.
7th row [K1, p1] twice, k3, * p1, C4F, p1, k7(9:11); rep from * once more, [p1, k1] twice.
8th row As 6th row.
9th row [K1, p1] twice, k3, * p1, k4, p1, k7(9:11); rep from * once more, [p1, k1] twice.
10th to 13th rows Rep 6th to 9th rows once more.
14th row [K1, p1] twice, * p7(9:11), k1, p4, k1; rep from * once more, p7.
15th row K7, * p1, C4F, p1, k7(9:11); rep from * once more, [p1, k1] twice.
16th row As 14th row.
17th row K7, * p1, k4, p1, k7(9:11); rep from * once more, [p1, k1] twice.
The last 4 rows, form the st st and cable patt with seed st front band. Patt 7(9:11) rows.
Place pocket
Next row (right side) K7, p1, k4, p1, k2(3:4), sl next 16(18:20)sts onto a holder and work [k5(6:7), p1, k4, p1, k5(6:7)] across 16(18:20) sts of first pocket lining, k2(3:4), [p1, k1] twice.

Cont in patt as set, keeping 4 sts at front edge in seed st, until left front measures 6¼(7:7½)in/16(17.5:19)cm from cast on edge, ending with a wrong side row.
Work straight in cable and seed st patt as given for 1st to 4th patt rows, until left front measures 9¾(11:11¾)in/25(28:30)cm from cast on edge, ending with a right side row.
Shape neck
Next row (wrong side) Bind off 7 sts in seed st, patt to end.
Dec one st at neck edge on every foll row until 21(23:25) sts rem.
Work straight until left front measures same as Back to shoulder, ending with a wrong side row.
Bind off rem 21(23:25) sts, working 2 sts tog across cables.
Mark the position for 7 buttons, the first ½in/1cm from cast on edge, the 7th, ½in/1cm below neck shaping with the rem 5 spaced evenly between.

Right Front

Work buttonholes to correspond with button markers on Left Front as follows:
Buttonhole row (right side) K1, p1, yrn, p2tog, patt to end.
With US 8(5mm) needles, cast on 37(41:45) sts.
1st row (right side) K1, [p1, k1] 5(6:7) times, p1, k4, [p1, k1] 4(5:6) times, p1, k4, [p1, k1] 4 times.
2nd row [K1, p1] 3 times, k2, p4, k2, [p1, k1] 3(4:5) times, k1, p4, k2, [p1, k1] 5(6:7) times.
3rd row K1, [p1, k1] 5(6:7) times, p1, C4F, [p1, k1] 4(5:6) times, p1, C4F, [p1, k1] 4 times.
4th row As 2nd row.
5th row As 1st row.
6th row [K1, p1] twice, p3, *k1, p4, k1, p7(9:11); rep from * once more, [p1, k1] twice.
7th row [K1, p1] twice, * k7(9:11), p1, C4F, p1; rep from * once more, k3, [p1, k1] twice.
8th row As 6th row.
9th row [K1, p1] twice, * k7(9:11), p1, k4, p1; rep from * once more, k3, [p1, k1] twice.

10th to 13th rows Rep 6th to 9th rows once more.

14th row P7, * k1, p4, k1, p7(9:11); rep from * once more, [p1, k1] twice.

15th row [K1, p1] twice, * k7(9:11), p1, C4F, p1; rep from * once more, k7.

16th row As 14th row.

17th row [K1, p1] twice, * k7(9:11), p1, k4, p1; rep from * once more, k7.

The last 4 rows, form the st st and cable patt with seed st front band. Patt 7(9:11) rows.

Place pocket

Next row (right side) [K1, p1] twice, k2(3:4), sl next 16(18:20) sts onto a holder and work [k5(6:7), p1, k4, p1, k5(6:7)] across 16(18:20) sts of second pocket lining, k2(3:4), p1, k4, p1, k7.

Cont in patt as set, keeping 4 sts at front edge in seed st, until right front measures 6¼(7:7½)in/16(17.5:19)cm from cast on edge, ending with a wrong side row.

Work straight in cable and seed st patt as given for 1st to 4th patt rows, until right front measures 9¾(11:11¾)in/25(28:30)cm from cast on edge, ending with a wrong side row.

Shape neck

Next row (right side) Bind off 7 sts in seed st, patt to end. Dec one st at neck edge on every foll row until 21(23:25) sts rem.

Work straight until right front measures same as Back to shoulder, ending with a right side row.

Bind off rem 21(23:25) sts, working 2 sts tog across cables.

Sleeves

Using US 8(5mm) needles cast on 33(37:37) sts.

1st row (right side) [K1, p1] 4(5:5) times, k4, [p1, k1] 4 times, p1, k4, [p1, k1] 4(5:5) times.

2nd row [K1, p1] 3(4:4) times, k2, p4, k2, [p1, k1] 3 times, k1, p4, k2, [p1, k1] 3(4:4) times.

3rd row [K1, p1] 4(5:5) times, C4F, [p1, k1] 4 times, p1, C4F, [p1, k1] 4(5:5) times.

4th row As 2nd row.

These 4 rows form the seed st and cable patt.

Work in patt, inc one st at each end of the 5th and every foll 5th row until there are 49(55:61) sts, taking inc sts into seed st.

Cont straight until sleeve measures 6¼(7:9)in/16(18:23)cm from cast on edge, ending with a right side row.

Working 2 sts tog across cables, bind off in patt.

Pocket Tops

With right side facing and US 8(5mm) needles, work in seed stitch across 16(18:20) sts from pocket stitch holder. Work a further 3 rows, bind off.

Collar

Join shoulder seams.

With right side facing and US 8(5mm) needles, starting 3 sts in from front edge, pick up and k19(19:21) sts up right front neck shaping, 29(31:33) sts across center back and k19(19:21) sts down left front neck to 3 sts from front edge. 67(69:75) sts.

Seed st 1 row.

Next 2 rows Seed st to last 19 sts, turn.

Next 2 rows Seed st to last 14 sts, turn.

Next 2 rows Seed st to last 9 sts, turn.

Next 2 rows Seed st to last 4 sts, turn.

Next row Seed st across all sts.

Seed st 12 rows.

Bind off in seed st.

Finish

With center of sleeve top to shoulder, sew on sleeves. Join side and sleeve seams. Sew on buttons.

hat with topknot and socks

A neat stockinette stitch beanie hat with garter stitch earflaps is teamed with a pair of matching socks.

Measurements
Socks:
To fit   4¼in/11cm foot length
Hat:
To fit ages   3-6   6-12   mths

Materials
Socks: One 50g/2oz ball of Debbie Bliss merino double knitting in Main shade (M) and small amount in Contrast shade (C).
Set of four US 6(4mm) double pointed knitting needles.
Hat: One 50g/2oz ball of Debbie Bliss merino double knitting in Main shade (M) and small amount in Contrast shade (C).
Pair of US 6(4mm) knitting needles.
Two US 6(4mm) double pointed knitting needles.

Gauge
22 sts and 30 rows to 4in/10cm square in st st using US 6(4mm) needles.

Abbreviations See page 7.

SOCKS
To make
With US 6(4mm) double pointed needles and C, cast on 32 sts.
Arrange sts on needles as follows: first 16 sts on first needle, next 8 sts on second needle and last 8 sts on third needle.
P 4 rounds.
Change to M.
P 10 rounds.
K 1 round.
P 2 rounds.
Next round [P2, k2] to end.

Rep the last round 9 times more.

K 4 rounds.

Shape heel

Working on first set of 16 sts only, beg with a k row, work 12 rows in st st.

Next row K10, skpo, turn.

Next row Sl1, p4, p2tog, turn.

Next row Sl1, k4, skpo, turn.

Next row Sl1, p4, p2tog, turn.

Rep the last 2 rows 3 times more.

Next round On first needle, K6, pick up and k6 sts down heel edge, m1, k2, on second needle, k9, on third needle, k5, m1, pick up and k6 sts up heel edge. 36 sts.

Next round K12, k2tog, k14, skpo, k6.

K 1 round.

Next round K11, k2tog, k14, skpo, k5.

K 1 round.

Next round K10, k2tog, k14, skpo, k4. 30 sts.

K 9 rounds.

Next round K8, k2tog, k1, skpo, k10, k2tog, k1, skpo, k2.

K 1 round.

Next round K7, k2tog, k1, skpo, k8, k2tog, k1, skpo, k1.

K 1 round.

Cont to dec in this way, rearranging sts on needles if necessary and working 2 sts less between groups of decs on every alt round, until 14 sts rem, then dec as set on next 2 rounds. 6 sts.

Break yarn, thread through rem sts, pull up and secure.

HAT

Earflaps (make 2)

With US 6(4mm) needles and M, cast on 15 sts.

K 1 row.

Next row K7, m1, k1, m1, k7.

K 1 row.

Next row K8, m1, k1, m1, k8.

K 1 row.

Cont in garter st, inc 1 st at each side of center st on every

foll alt row until there are 27 sts.

Bind off knitwise.

Fold cast on edge in half and join seam.

Hat

With US 6(4mm) needles and M, cast on 10(12) sts, pick up and k13 sts across row ends of first earflap, cast on 39(43) sts, pick up and k13 sts across row ends of second earflap, cast on 10(12) sts. 85(93) sts.

K 3 rows.

Beg with a k row, work 18(22) rows in st st and dec 0(1) st in center of last row. 85(92) sts.

Shape top

Next row [K2tog, k5] 12(13) times, k1. 73(79) sts.

Cont in st st, work 3 rows.

Next row [K2tog, k4] 12(13) times, k1. 61(66) sts.

Work 3 rows.

Next row [K2tog, k3] 12(13) times, k1. 49(53) sts.

P 1 row.

Next row [K2tog, k2] 12(13) times, k1. 37(40) sts.

P 1 row.

Next row [K2tog, k1] 12(13) times, k1. 25(27) sts.

P 1 row.

Next row [K2tog] 12(13) times, k1. 13(14) sts.

P 1 row.

Next row [K2tog] 6(7) times, k1(0). 7 sts.

P 1 row.

With two US 6(4mm) double pointed needles and C, k 1 row. Slide these 7 sts to the opposite end of the same needle, place needle in left hand and bringing yarn firmly from last st to first st, k7 sts.

Repeat this row until a tube of approx 5in/13cm has been worked.

Next row K2tog, k3tog, k2tog, cut yarn, thread end through rem 3 sts, pull up and secure.

Finish

Join back seam. Tie top extension in a knot.

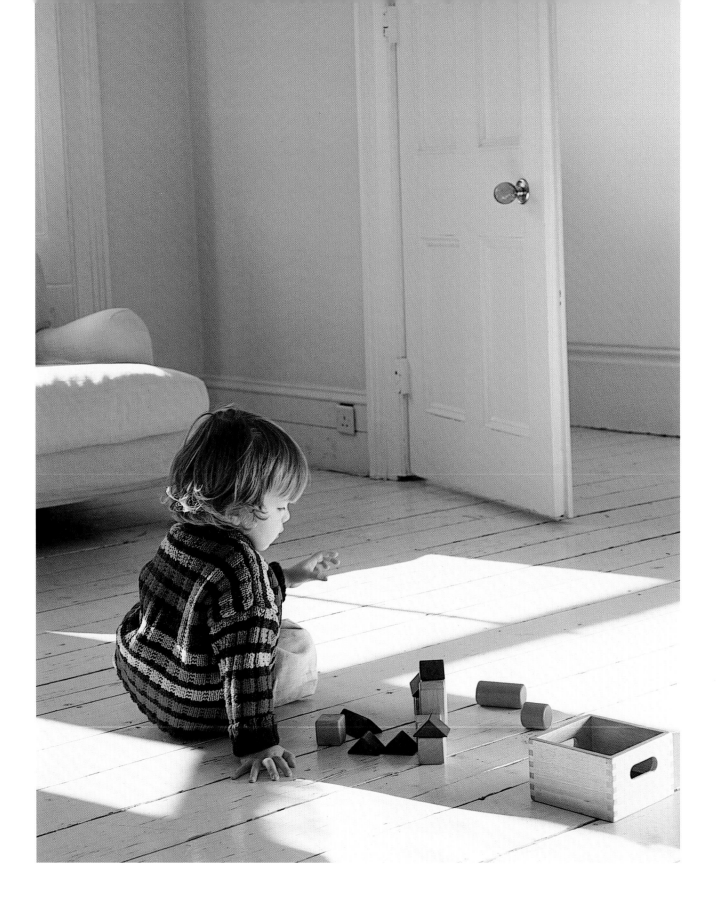

striped sweater

Here's an easy-to-knit, ribbed sweater with a roll collar. As every wrong side row is purled, this is a rib pattern that knits up quickly.

Measurements

To fit ages

1-2	2-3	3-4	years

Actual measurements

Chest

26	30	34	in
66	76	86	cm

Length

12½	14¼	16½	in
32	36	42	cm

Sleeve seam (with cuff turned back)

7½	8¾	9¾	in
19	22	25	cm

Materials

3(4:4) 50g/2oz balls of Debbie Bliss merino aran in Main shade Navy (M) and one 50g/2oz ball in each of Turquoise (A), Red (B), Fuchsia (C), Lilac (D), Green (E) and Pale Turquoise (F).
Pair each of US 7(4½mm) and US 8 (5mm) knitting needles.

Gauge

19 sts and 24 rows to 4in/10cm square over pattern using US 8 (5mm) needles.

Abbreviations See page 7.

Back

With US 7(4½mm) needles and A, cast on 63(73:83) sts.
1st row (right side) K3, [p2, k3] to end.
2nd row P to end.
These 2 rows form the patt. Rep 1st row once more.
Change to US 8(5mm) needles.
Beg with a 2nd patt row, cont in patt working stripe patt as follows: ** 4 rows M, 6 rows B, 4 rows M, 6 rows C, 4 rows M, 6 rows D, 4 rows M, 6 rows E, 4 rows M, 6 rows F, 4 rows M, 6 rows A, until back measures 12½(14¼:16½)in/ 32(36:42)cm from cast on edge, ending with a wrong side row.

Shape shoulders

Bind off 9(11:13) sts at beg of next 4 rows.
Leave rem 27(29:31) sts on a holder.

Front

Work as given for Back until front measures 10¾(12¼:14½)in/ 27(31:37)cm, ending with a wrong side row.

Shape neck

Next row Patt 26(30:34), turn and work on these sts for first side of neck.
Dec one st at neck edge on next 8 rows. 18(22:26) sts.
Cont straight until front measures same as Back to shoulder, ending at side edge.

Shape shoulder

Bind off 9(11:13) sts at beg of next row.
Work 1 row. Bind off rem 9(11:13) sts.
With right side facing, slip center 11(13:15) sts onto a holder, rejoin yarn to rem sts, and patt to end.
Complete to match first side.

Sleeves

With US 7(4½mm) needles and A, cast on 38(43:43) sts.

1st rib row P3, [k2, p3] to end.

2nd rib row K3, [p2, k3] to end.

Rep 1st rib row once more. Change to M.

Work a further 1½in/4cm in rib for cuff, ending with a 1st rib row.

Beg with a 1st rib row, so reversing cuff, work a further 2in/5cm, ending with a 2nd rib row.

Change to US 8(5mm) needles.

Work in patt and stripe sequence as given for Back from **, inc one st at each end of 2nd and every foll 4th row until there are 52(59:63) sts.

Work straight until sleeve measures 9½(10¾:11¾)in/ 24(27:30)cm from cast on edge, ending with a wrong side row. Bind off in patt.

Neckband

Join right shoulder.

With right side facing, US 7(4½mm) needles and M, pick up and k17(16:18) sts down left front neck, patt across 11(13:15) sts at center front, pick up and k16(14:17) sts up right front neck, then patt across 27(29:31) sts at center back. 71(72:81) sts.

1st rib row (wrong side) P0(1:2), [k2, p3] to last 1(1:4) sts, k1(1:2), p0(0:2).

2nd rib row K0(0:2), p1(1:2), [k3, p2] to last 0(1:2) sts, k0(1:2). Rib 8 rows.

Next row K0(1:2), [p2, k3] to last 1(1:4) sts, p1(1:2), k0(0:2).

Next row P0(0:2), k1(1:2), [p3, k2] to last 0(1:2) sts, p0(1:2).

Work a further 5 rows as set. Change to A. P 1 row.

Rib a further 3 rows. Bind off in rib.

Finish

Join left shoulder and neckband seam, reversing seam for last 2in/5cm of neckband. Sew on sleeves, placing center of bound off edge to shoulder seam. Join side and sleeve seams, reversing seam on lower half of cuffs. Turn back cuffs.

bear in lamb sleep suit

Here's a small, tired bear in an all-in-one lamb sleep suit.
The yarn is soft to the touch but hardwearing.

Measurements
Bear approximately 7in/18cm tall.

Materials
Bear: One 50g/2oz ball of Debbie
Bliss merino double knitting in Camel
and small amount in Brown for
embroidery.
Pair of US 2(2³⁄₄mm) knitting needles.
Stuffing.
Sleep suit: One 50g/2oz ball of
Debbie Bliss wool/cotton in Main
shade (M) Cream and small amount
in Contrast shade (C) Black.
Pair US 3(3¹⁄₄mm) knitting needles.
3 small buttons.

Gauges
32 sts and 40 rows to 4in/10cm
square over st st using merino
double knitting and US 2(2³⁄₄mm)
needles.
25 sts and 34 rows to 4in/10cm
square over st st using wool/cotton
and US 3(3¹⁄₄mm) needles.

Abbreviations See page 7.

Note Bear is worked throughout in
merino double knitting and US 2
(2³⁄₄mm) needles and Sleep Suit is
worked throughout in wool/cotton
and US 3(3¹⁄₄mm) needles.

BEAR
Legs (make 2)
Cast on 26 sts. Beg with a k row, work 5 rows in st st.
Next row P13, turn.
Cont in st st, work on this set of sts only. Dec one st at beg
of next row and foll alt row, then at end of foll row. 10 sts.
Break off yarn and rejoin at inside edge to second set of 13
sts, p to end.
Dec one st at end of next row and foll alt row, then at beg of
foll row. 10 sts.
K 1 row across both sets of sts. 20 sts.
Work 10 rows.
Next row P10, turn.
Work on this set of sts only. Dec one st at each end of next 2
rows. 6 sts. Work 1 row. Bind off.
Rejoin yarn to rem sts and complete as first side.

Soles (make 2)
Cast on 3 sts. K 1 row.
Work in st st, inc one st at each end of next 2 rows and foll
alt row. 9 sts.
Work 6 rows straight.
Dec one st at each end of next row and foll alt row, then on
foll row. 3 sts.
P 1 row. Bind off.

Arms (make 2)
* Cast on 4 sts.
Beg with a k row, work in st st, inc one st at each end of 3rd
row and foll alt row. 8 sts. P 1 row. * Break off yarn.
Work from * to *.

K 1 row across both sets of sts. 16 sts.

Cont in st st, inc one st at each end of 2nd row and foll 4th row. 20 sts.

Work 9 rows straight.

Next row K10, turn.

Work on this set of sts only. Dec one st at each end of next 2 rows. 6 sts.

Work 1 row. Bind off.

Rejoin yarn to rem sts and complete to match first side.

Body (make 2)

* Cast on 3 sts. K 1 row.

Work in st st, inc one st at each end of next 2 rows and 2 foll alt rows. 11 sts. * Break off yarn.

Work from * to *.

P 1 row across both sets of sts. 22 sts.

Work 12 rows straight.

Dec one st at each end of next row and 2 foll 3rd rows, then on foll alt row. 14 sts.

P 1 row. Bind off.

Back Head

Cast on 3 sts. K 1 row.

Work in st st, inc one st at each end of next 2 rows, then at end of 3 foll rows.

Work 1 row.

Inc one st at beg of next row. 11 sts.

K 1 row.

Break off yarn.

Cast on 3 sts. K 1 row.

Work in st st, inc one st at each end of next 2 rows, then at beg of 3 foll rows.

Work 1 row.

Inc one st at end of next row. 11 sts. K 1 row.

P 1 row across both sets of sts. 22 sts.

Work 6 rows straight.

Next row K11, turn.

Work on this set of sts only. Dec one st at each end of next row.

Work 1 row.

Dec one st at end of next 3 rows. Mark end of last row.

Dec one st at each end of next row. 4 sts.

Work 1 row.

Bind off.

Rejoin yarn at inside edge to rem sts and k to end.

Dec one st at each end of next row.

Work 1 row.

Dec one st at beg of next 3 rows. Mark beg of last row.

Dec one st at each end of next row. 4 sts.

Work 1 row. Bind off.

Right Side Head

Cast on 6 sts. K 1 row.

P 1 row, inc one st at beg.

Work in st st, inc one st at each end of next row, then at beg of 4 foll rows.

Inc one st at end of next row and at beg of foll row. 15 sts.

Work 5 rows straight. Mark end of last row.

Bind off 2 sts at beg of next row.

Dec one st at end of next row and beg of foll row.

* Dec one st at each end of next row and at beg of foll row.*

Rep from * to *. 5 sts.

Work 1 row. Mark beg of last row. Bind off.

Left Side Head

Work as given for Right Side Head, reversing shapings by reading p for k and k for p.

Head Gusset

Cast on 11 sts.

Beg with a k row, work 4 rows in st st.

Dec one st at each end of next row and foll alt row, then on foll row.

Work 2 rows.

Dec one st at each end of next row.

Work 1 row.

K3tog and fasten off.

Ears (make 4)

Cast on 6 sts. Work 3 rows in st st.
Dec one st at each end of next 2 rows. Bind off.

Finish

Join instep, top and back leg seams, leaving an opening.
Sew in soles. Stuff and close opening. Join arm seams,
leaving an opening. Stuff and close opening. Join center
seam on each body piece. Join body pieces together, leaving
bound off edge open. Stuff and gather open edge, pull up
and secure. Join sides of head from cast on edge to first
marker. Sew in head gusset, placing point at center front
seam and cast on edge in line with second marker on sides
of head. Join center seams of back head, then sew to front
head, matching markers and leaving cast on edge open.
Stuff and gather open edge, pull up and secure. Sew head to
body. Attach yarn about ½in/1cm below top of one arm,
thread yarn through body at shoulder position, then attach
other arm, pull yarn tightly and thread through body again
in same place, then attach yarn to first arm again and fasten
off. Attach legs at hip position in same way as arms. Join
paired ear pieces together and sew them in place.
Embroider face features in Brown.

SLEEP SUIT

Left Leg

With C, cast on 35 sts.
Beg with a k row, work 8 rows in st st.

Shape instep

Next row K26, k2tog, turn.
Next row Sl 1, p3, p2tog, turn.
Next row Sl 1, k3, k2tog, turn.
Next row Sl 1, p3, p2tog, turn.
Next row Sl 1, k3, k2tog, k to end.
Next row P9, p2tog, p to end. 29 sts.
** **Next row** K4, [k twice in next st, k6] 3 times, k twice in
next st, k3. 33 sts.
Change to M. Work 11 rows straight.

Shape crotch

Dec one st at each end of next 2 rows. 29 sts. **
Leave these sts on a spare needle.

Right Leg

With C, cast on 35 sts.
Beg with a k row, work 8 rows in st st.

Shape instep

Next row K12, k2tog, turn.
Next row Sl 1, p3, p2tog, turn.
Next row Sl 1, k3, k2tog, turn.
Next row Sl 1, p3, p2tog, turn.
Next row Sl 1, k3, k2tog, k to end.
Next row P23, p2tog, p to end. 29 sts.
Work as Left Leg from ** to **.
Next row K28, k last st tog with first st of Left Leg, k rem
sts. 57 sts.
Work 3 rows straight.

Shape front opening

Bind off 3 sts at beg of next 2 rows. 51 sts.
Work 10 rows straight.

Right Front

Next row K12, turn.
Work on this set of sts only for 5 rows.

Shape neck

Bind off 2 sts at beg of next row.
Dec one st at neck edge on next 3 rows.
Work 3 rows straight. Bind off.

Back

Rejoin yarn to rem sts, k27, turn.
Work on this set of sts only for 9 rows.

Shape neck

Next row K8, bind off next 11 sts, k to end.
Work on last set of 8 sts only.
Dec one st at neck edge on next row.
Work 1 row.
Bind off.
Rejoin yarn to rem 8 sts and complete as first side.

Left Front

Rejoin yarn to rem sts and complete as Right Front, reversing neck shaping.

Arms (make 2)

With M, cast on 28 sts. Beg with a k row, work in st st.
Dec one st at each end of 5th row and foll 4th row. 24 sts.
Work 3 rows straight.
Change to C.
Next row K2tog, k3, sl 1, k2tog, psso, k8, sl 1, k2tog, psso, k3, k2tog.
P 1 row.
Next row K3, sl 1, k2tog, psso, k6, sl 1, k2tog, psso, k3.
P 1 row.
Next row K2, sl 1, k2tog, psso, k4, sl 1, k2tog, psso, k2.
Next row P1, p3tog, p2, p3tog, p1. Bind off.

Soles (make 2)

With C, cast on 4 sts.
Beg with a k row, work in st st.
Inc one st at each end of 2nd, 3rd and 5th rows. 10 sts.
Work 7 rows straight.
Dec one st at each end of next row, foll alt row and foll row. 4 sts.
Work 1 row. Bind off.

Neckband and Hood

Join shoulder seams.
With right side facing and M, pick up and k10 sts up right front neck, 3 sts down right back neck, 11 sts at center back, 3 sts up left back neck and 10 sts down left front neck. 37 sts.
1st rib row K1, [p1, k1] to end.
2nd rib row P1, [k1, p1] to end.
Rib 1 row more.
Next row Rib 4 and slip these 4 sts onto a safety pin, k5, [k twice in next st, k8] twice, k twice in next st, k5, turn, slip the last 4 sts onto safety pin. 32 sts.
Beg with a p row, work 15 rows in st st.

Next row K15, k2tog, k4, k3tog, turn.
Next row Sl 1, p9, p3tog, turn.
* **Next row** Sl 1, k9, k2tog, turn.
Next row Sl 1, p9, p2tog, turn. *
Rep from * to * once.
** **Next row** Sl 1, k9, k3tog, turn.
Next row Sl 1, p9, p3tog, turn. **
Rep from * to * once, then from ** to ** once.
Leave rem 13 sts on a needle.
With right side facing, sl 4 sts from right side of neckband onto needles, pick up and k11 sts along side of hood, k2tog, k9, skpo across sts on needle, pick up and k11 sts down other side of hood, then rib the 4 sts on safety pin. 41 sts.
Rib 2 rows. Bind off in rib.

Buttonhole Band

With right side facing, pick up and k20 sts along right edge of front opening to top of hood edging.
Work 2 rows in p1, k1 rib.
Buttonhole row P1, k1, [yf, k2tog, rib 4] 3 times.
Rib 2 rows. Bind off in rib.

Button Band

Work to match Buttonhole Band omitting buttonholes.

Ears (make 2)

With C, cast on 14 sts.
Beg with a k row, work in st st.
Work 4 rows.
Next row K2tog, k to last 2 sts, skpo. P 1 row.
Dec one st at each end of next and foll 3 alt rows. Bind off.

Finish

Join leg, crotch, and center front seams. Sew in soles. Join arm seams, leaving cast on edge free. Sew in arms. Lap buttonhole band over button band and catch row end edges to base of front opening. Sew on buttons. Fold cast on edge of ears in half and secure, then sew in place to hood.

dressing gown

This is a classic dressing gown. It is knitted in soft cashmerino, for the ultimate in baby luxury.

Measurements

To fit ages

6	12	18	24	mths

Actual measurements

Chest

24¾	26½	28¼	30	in
63	67	72	76	cm

Length

17¾	20	22	24¾	in
45	51	56	63	cm

Sleeve seam (with cuff turned back)

8¾	9½	10¼	11½	in
22	24	26	29	cm

Materials

6(7:8:9) 50g/2oz balls of Debbie Bliss cashmerino aran in Lilac (M) and one 50g/2oz ball in Mauve (C).
Pair each of US 6(4mm) and US 8(5mm) knitting needles.

Gauge

18 sts and 24 rows to 4in/10cm square over st st using US 8(5mm) needles.

Abbreviations

kfb = k into front and back of next st.
See also page 7.

Back

With US 6(4mm) needles and M, cast on 67(73:79:83) sts.
Beg with a k row, work in st st.
Work 6 rows.
P 1 row for hemline.
Change to US 8(5mm) needles.
Beg with a p row, cont in st st.
Work 37(43:51:57) rows.
Dec row (right side) K3, k2tog, k to last 5 sts, skpo, k3.
Cont in st st, dec one st as set at each end of 4(5:6:6) foll 6th rows. 57(61:65:69) sts.
Work 13(13:13:19) rows.
Shape armholes
Bind off 2 sts at beg of next 2 rows.
Dec one st at each end of next and 3 foll right side rows. 45(49:53:57) sts.
Work 25(27:27:29) rows. Bind off.

Pocket Linings (make 2)

With US 8(5mm) needles and M, cast on 12(14:16:16) sts.
Beg with a k row, work in st st for 14(16:18:18) rows.
Leave sts on a holder.

Left Front

With US 6(4mm) needles and M, cast on 34(38:42:44) sts.
Beg with a k row, work in st st.
Work 6 rows.
P 1 row for hemline.
Change to US 8(5mm) needles.
Next row (wrong side) Cast on 14 sts, p these sts, p to end.
48(52:56:58) sts.

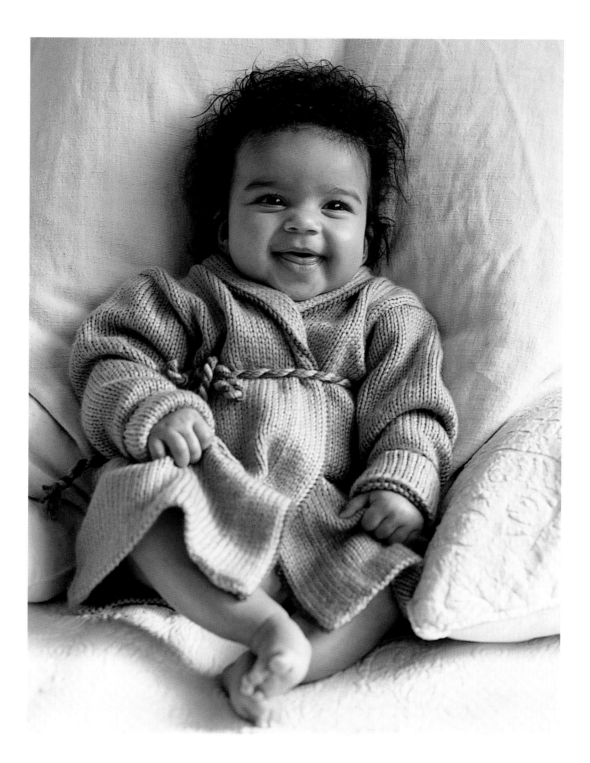

Beg with a k row, work in st st.

Work 36(42:50:56) rows.

Dec row (right side) K3, k2tog, k to end.

Cont in st st and dec in this way at beg of foll 6th row. 46(50:54:56) sts.

P 1 row.

Pocket opening row (right side) K11(12:13:14), slip next 12(14:16:16) sts onto a holder and k12(14:16:16) sts of first pocket lining, k23(24:25:26).

Work 3 rows.

Dec as before at beg of next row and 2(3:4:4) foll 6th rows. 43(46:49:51) sts.

Work 13(13:13:19) rows.

Shape armhole and collar

Next row (right side) Bind off 2 sts, k to last 2 sts, kfb, k1.

P 1 row.

Next row K3, k2tog, k to last 2 sts, kfb, k1.

Rep the last 2 rows 3 times more. 42(45:48:50) sts.

Work 3 rows.

Next row K to last 2 sts, kfb, k1.

Rep the last 4 rows 1(3:5:6) times more. 44(49:54:57) sts.

Work 17(11:3:1) rows.

Shape shoulder

Next row (right side) Bind off 16(17:18:19) sts, k to end. 28(32:36:38) sts.

Cont on these sts until collar reaches center back neck.

Leave sts on a holder.

Right Front

With US 6(4mm) needles and M, cast on 34(38:42:44) sts.

Beg with a k row, work in st st.

Work 6 rows.

Next row (right side) Cast on 14 sts, p these sts, p to end. 48(52:56:58) sts.

Change to US 8(5mm) needles.

Beg with a p row, work in st st.

Work 37(43:51:57) rows.

Dec row (right side) K to last 5 sts, skpo, k3.

Cont in st st and dec in this way at end of foll 6th row. 46(50:54:56) sts.

P 1 row.

Pocket opening row (right side) K23(24:25:26), slip next 12(14:16:16) sts onto a holder and k12(14:16:16) sts of second pocket lining, k11(12:13:14).

Work 3 rows.

Dec as before at end of next row and 2(3:4:4) foll 6th rows. 43(46:49:51) sts.

Work 13(13:13:19) rows.

Shape armhole and collar

Next row (right side) Kfb, k to end.

Next row Bind off 2 sts, p to end.

Next row Kfb, k to last 5 sts, skpo, k3.

P 1 row.

Rep the last 2 rows 3 times more. 42(45:48:50) sts.

Work 2 rows.

Next row Kfb, k to end.

P 1 row.

Rep the last 4 rows 1(3:5:6) times more. 44(49:54:57) sts.

Work 17(11:3:1) rows.

Shape shoulder

Next row (wrong side) Bind off 16(17:18:19) sts, p to end. 28(32:36:38) sts.

Cont on these sts until collar reaches center back neck. Leave sts on a holder.

Sleeves

With US 8(5mm) needles and M, cast on 29(31:33:35) sts.

Beg with a k row, work in st st.

Work 10(12:14:14) rows.

Change to US 6(4mm) needles.

P 1 row for hemline.

Beg with a p row, work in st st.

Work 9(11:13:13) rows.

Change to US 8(5mm) needles.

Work 2 rows.

Inc row (right side) K2, kfb, k to last 4 sts, kfb, k3.

Cont in st st, and inc one st at each end of 8(9:8:9) foll 6th rows. 47(51:51:55) sts.

Work 3(1:13:13) rows.

Shape top

Bind off 2 sts at beg of next 2 rows.

Next row (right side) K3, k2tog, k to last 5 sts, skpo, k3.

P 1 row.

Rep the last 2 rows 3 times more. 35(39:39:43) sts.

Bind off 4 sts at beg of next 4 rows. 19(23:23:27) sts.

Bind off.

Pocket Tops

With right side facing, US 8(5mm) needles and C, k12(14:16:16) sts from holder.

Bind off purlwise.

Front Edgings

Right front

With US 6(4mm) needles and C, beg at lower edge, working between 7th and 8th sts from edge and inserting needle through fabric each time, pick up and k one st from each row up right front edge. Note that the same line is kept throughout so at the collar the pick up will be between the 14th(16th:18th:19th) and 15th(17th:19th:20th) sts from edge. Bind off knitwise.

Left front

Work to match right front but beg at collar edge, working between 14th(16th:18th:19th) and 15th(17th:19th:20th) sts, so ending between 7th and 8th sts at lower edge.

Bind off purlwise.

Cuff Edgings

Fold hem onto wrong side.

With cast on edge facing, US 8(5mm) needles and C, pick up and k one st from each st along hemline.

Bind off purlwise.

Tie Belt

Cut three 4½yd/4m lengths each of M and C. Knot 3 ends of M to 3 ends of C, smooth yarn out making sure that there are no tangles, and knot the other ends together to make a long loop of yarn. With knots lined up in the center, attach one end to a fixed point, and twist the other end until the yarn springs back on itself. Hold the knots firmly and bring the other two ends together, they will twist around each other to make a two color cord. Knot ends to secure, then leaving 1in/2.5cm tassels, trim cord to 39½(41½:43¼:45¼)in/ 100(105:110:115)cm.

Finish

Matching sts, join shoulders. Graft sts from holders for center back collar. Sew row ends of undercollar to back neck. Turn facings in to wrong side, join cast on sts at lower edges of fronts, slip st facings in place and sew row ends of collar to back neck. Slip st pocket linings in place. Join side and sleeve seams. Turn up hems. Fold back cuffs.

Make two 2¼in/6cm lengths of crochet chain and sew to side seams at waist level. Thread belt through loops and tie at front.

special

beaded fair isle cardigan

A very special cardigan with a delicately shaded Fair Isle yoke enhanced by sewing on toning beads. See page 90 for the matching shoes.

Measurements

To fit ages

3-6	6-9	9-12	mths

Actual measurements

Chest

19¾	22	24½	in
50	56	62	cm

Length to shoulder

8¾	9½	10¼	in
22	24	26	cm

Sleeve length

5½	6¼	7	in
14	16	18	cm

Material

3(4:5) 50g/2oz balls of Debbie Bliss wool/cotton in Main shade (M) Pale Pink.
One 50g/2oz ball each in Khaki, Dark Aqua, Pale Aqua, White, Fuchsia and Yellow.
Pair each of US 2(2¾mm) and US 3(3¼mm) knitting needles.
US 2(2¾mm), US 2-3(3mm) and US 3(3¼mm) circular needles.
6 buttons.
74(82:90) small blue glass beads and 37(41:45) small fuchsia glass beads.

Gauge

25 sts and 34 rows to 4in/10cm square over st st using US 3(3¼mm) needles.

Abbreviations See page 7.

Note Read chart from right to left on odd-numbered (k) rows and from left to right on even-numbered (p) rows. When working in patt, strand yarn not in use loosely across wrong side to keep fabric elastic.

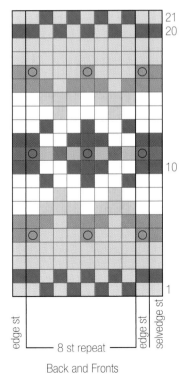

Back and Fronts

Key

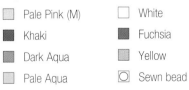

- ▨ Pale Pink (M)
- ◼ Khaki
- ▨ Dark Aqua
- ▨ Pale Aqua
- ☐ White
- ◼ Fuchsia
- ▨ Yellow
- ○ Sewn bead

Back and Fronts

Using US 2(2¾mm) needles and M, cast on 125(141:157) sts.

1st rib row P1, * k1, p1; rep from * to end.

2nd rib row K1, * p1, k1; rep from * to end.

Rep the last 2 rows 2(2:3) times more.

Change to US 3(3¼mm) needles.

Beg with a k row, cont in st st until work measures 4¾(5:5½)in/12(13:14)cm from cast on edge, ending with a wrong side row.

Divide for Back and Fronts

Next row K31(35:39), leave these sts on a holder for right front, k next 63(71:79) and leave these sts on a holder for back, k to end.

Left Front

Work straight on last set of 31(35:39) sts for 2(4:6) rows, so ending with a p row.

Yoke shaping

Bind off 6 sts at beg of next row, 3 sts at beg of 3 foll alt rows, then 2 sts on 3(4:5) foll alt rows.

Dec one st on every foll alt row until 3(5:7) sts rem.

Cont straight until front measures 8¾(9½:10¼)in/22(24:26)cm from cast on edge, ending at armhole edge.

Shape shoulder

Bind off.

Back

With wrong side facing, rejoin yarn to next st on back holder, p63(71:79).

Work straight on these sts for 2(4:6) rows.

Yoke shaping

Next row (right side) K25(29:33), turn and work on these sts.

Bind off 3 sts at beg of next row, and 2 foll alt rows, then 2 sts on 3(4:5) foll alt rows.

Dec one st on every foll alt row until 3(5:7) sts rem.

Cont straight until front measures 8¾(9½:10¼)in/22(24:26)cm from cast on edge, ending at armhole edge.

Shape shoulder

Bind off.

With right side facing, slip center 13 sts onto a holder, rejoin

yarn to rem 25(29:33) sts, k to end.

P 1 row.

Complete to match first side.

Right Front

With wrong side facing, rejoin yarn to next st on right front holder, p to end.

Work straight on these 31(35:39) sts for 2(4:6) rows.

Yoke shaping

Bind off 6 sts at beg of next row, 3 sts at beg of 3 foll alt rows, then 2 sts on 3(4:5) foll alt rows. Dec one st on every foll alt row until 3(5:7) sts rem.

Cont straight until front measures 8¾(9½:10¼)in/22(24:26)cm from cast on edge, ending at armhole edge.

Shape shoulder

Bind off.

Yoke

Join shoulder seams.

With right side facing, US 3(3¼mm) circular needle and M, pick up and k41(45:50) sts up right front neck edge, 35(40:44) sts down right back neck edge, k across 13 sts from center back neck holder, pick up and k35(40:44) sts up left back neck edge and 41(45:50) sts down left front neck edge. 165(183:201) sts.

P 1 row.

Work 1st to 3rd Chart rows.

Dec row (4th Chart row) P5, p2tog, * p7, p2tog; rep from * to last 5 sts, p5. 147(163:179) sts.

Work 5th to 10th rows from Chart.

Change to US 2-3(3mm) circular needle.

Work 11th to 18th row from Chart.

Dec row (19th Chart row) K3, * k2tog, k2; rep from * to end. 111(123:135) sts.

Work 20th and 21st Chart rows.

Cont in M only. P 1 row.

Dec row K2, * k2tog, k1; rep from * to last 4 sts, k2tog, k2. 75(83:91) sts.

Change to US 2(2¾mm) circular needle.

1st rib row K1, * p1, k1; rep from * to end.

2nd rib row P1, * k1, p1; rep from * to end.
Rep the last 2 rows once more. Bind off.

Sleeves

With US 2(2¾mm) needles and M, cast on 36(40:44) sts.
Work 6(8:10) rows in k1, p1 rib.
Change to US 3(3¼mm) needles.
Beg with a k row, work in st st, inc one st at each end of the
3rd and every foll 4th row until there are 52(58:64) sts.
Cont straight until sleeve measures 5½(6¼:7)in/14(16:18)cm
from cast on edge, ending with a p row. Bind off.

Button band

With right side facing, US 2(2¾mm) needles and M, pick up
and k55(61:67) sts along left front edge.

Work 4 rows in rib as given for Back and Fronts.
Bind off in rib.

Buttonhole band

With right side facing, US 2(2¾mm) needles and M, pick up
and k55(61:67) sts along right front edge.
Work 1 row in rib as given for Back and Fronts.
Buttonhole row Rib 2, [rib 2tog, yf, rib 8(9:10) sts] 5 times,
rib 2tog, yf, rib 1(2:3).
Rib 2 rows.
Bind off in rib.

Finish

Join sleeve seams. Sew sleeves into armholes. Sew on
buttons. Sew beads to yoke where indicated on chart.

beaded fair isle shoes

Designed to match the beaded Fair Isle cardigan on page 86, these shoes would also make a perfect gift for a special baby.

Measurements
To fit ages   3-6   6-9   mths

Materials
One 50g/2oz ball of Debbie Bliss wool/cotton in Main shade (M) Pale Pink and small amounts of Khaki, Cream, Fuchsia and Yellow.
Pair of US 2(2¾mm) knitting needles.
34(40) small pink beads.
2 small buttons.

Gauge
28 sts and 40 rows to 4in/10cm square over st st using US 2(2¾mm) needles.

Abbreviations See page 7.

Note Read chart from right to left on right side rows and from left to right on wrong side rows. When working in patt, strand yarn not in use loosely across wrong side to keep fabric elastic.

Left Shoe

With US 2(2¾mm) needles and M, cast on 37(43) sts.

K 1 row.

1st row K1, [m1, k17(20), m1, k1] twice.

2nd and every foll alt row K.

3rd row K2, m1, k17(20), m1, k3, m1, k17(20), m1, k2.

5th row K3, m1, k17(20), m1, k5, m1, k17(20), m1, k3.

Cont in this way, inc 4 sts as set on every alt row until there are 61(71) sts.

K 1 row.

Next row (right side) K6(4), m1, [k7, m1] 7(9) times, k6(4). 69(81) sts.

P 1 row.

Beg with a k row, work 5 rows in st st from Chart.

P 1 row.

Next row K 8(7), k2tog, [k15(11), k2tog] 3(5) times, k8(7). 65(75) sts.

Next row P37(42), p2tog, turn.

Next row Sl 1, k9, skpo, turn.

Next row Sl 1, p9, p2tog, turn.

Rep last 2 rows 5(7) times more, then work first of the 2 rows again.

Next row Sl 1, p to end.

P 1 row.

Bind off purlwise, working 2 sts tog at each corner.

Join back and sole seam.

With right side facing, US 2(2¾mm) needles and M, and beg and ending 10 sts to either side of back seam, pick up and k21 sts along back heel edge.

K 1 row. **

Next row Cast on 20(23), k to end, turn and cast on 4 sts.

K 1 row.

Buttonhole row K2, yf, skpo, k to end.

K 2 rows.

Bind off.

Sew on button.

Sew beads to the center row of the Fair Isle band, as indicated on chart.

Right Shoe

Work as given for Left Shoe to **.

Next row Cast on 4 sts, k to end, turn and cast on 20(23) sts.

K 1 row.

Buttonhole row K to last 4 sts, k2tog, yf, k2.

K 2 rows.

Bind off.

Sew on button. Sew on beads as Left Shoe.

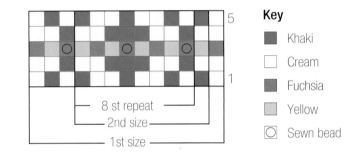

Key

- ■ Khaki
- □ Cream
- ▨ Fuchsia
- ▨ Yellow
- ⊙ Sewn bead

dress with lace edging

This vintage style dress has an easy-to-knit lace edging and an eyelet and ribbon tie neckline.

Measurements

To fit ages

6-12	12-18	18-24	24-36	mths

Actual measurements

Chest

20½	22	24½	26½	in
52	56	62	67	cm

Length to shoulder (excluding edging)

13¾	16½	17¾	19¼	in
35	42	45	50	cm

Sleeve length

7	8¾	9½	10¼	in
18	22	24	26	cm

Materials

5(6:7:8) 50g/2oz balls of Debbie Bliss wool/cotton.
Pair each of US 2(2¾mm) and US 3(3¼mm) knitting needles.
One US 2(2¾mm) circular knitting needle.
1 button.
24in/61cm narrow ribbon.

Gauge

25 sts and 34 rows to 4in/10cm square over st st using US 3(3¼mm) needles.

Abbreviations See page 7.

Back

With US 3(3¼mm) needles cast on 97(107:117:127) sts.
Beg with a k row, work in st st.
Work 6 rows.
Dec row (right side) K10(11:12:13), skpo, k to last 12(13:14:15) sts, k2tog, k10(11:12:13).
Work 7(9:9:11) rows.
Rep the last 8(10:10:12) rows until 81(89:97:107) sts rem.
Cont straight until back measures 9(11½:12½:13¾)in/23(29:31.5:35)cm from cast on edge, ending with a right side row.
Dec row P4(4:8:2), [p2tog, p4(3:3:3)] 12(16:16:20) times, p2tog, p3(3:7:3). 68(72:80:86) sts.
Change to US 2(2¾mm) needles.
K 6 rows.
Change to US 3(3¼mm) needles.
Cont straight until back measures 10¼(12½:13½:15)in/26(32:34:38)cm from cast on edge, ending with a p row.
Shape armholes
Bind off 4 sts at beg of next 2 rows.
Dec one st at each end of the next and every foll alt row until 42(48:54:58) sts rem.
P 1 row.
Back opening
Next row K21(24:27:29) sts, turn and work on these sts for first side of back opening.
Next row K2, p to end.
Next row K to end.
Repeat the last 2 rows until back measures 13(15¾:17:18½)in/33(40:43:48)cm from cast on edge, ending with a wrong side row.

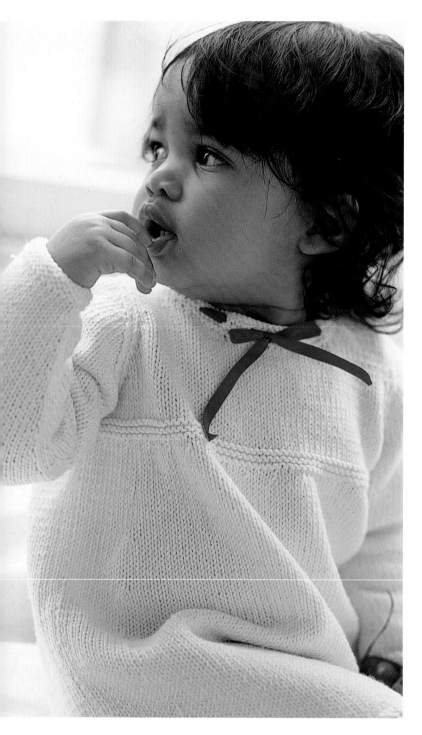

Shape neck

Next row K to last 8(8:10:10) sts, leave these sts on a holder, turn.

Next row Bind off 3 sts, p to end.

K 1 row.

Next row Bind off 2(3:2:3) sts, p to end.

Beg with a k row, work 2 rows st st.

Shape shoulder

Bind off rem 8(10:12:13) sts.

With right side facing, rejoin yarn to rem sts, k to end.

Next row P to last 2 sts, k2.

Next row K to end.

Repeat the last 2 rows until back measures 13(15¾:17:18½)in/33(40:43:48)cm from cast on edge, ending with a wrong side row.

Shape neck

Next row K8(8:10:10) sts, leave these sts on a holder, k to end.

P 1 row.

Next row Bind off 3 sts, k to end.

P 1 row.

Next row Bind off 2(3:2:3) sts, k to end.

Beg with a p row, work 2 rows st st.

Shape shoulder

Bind off rem 8(10:12:13) sts.

Front

Work as given for Back until front measures 11¾(14½:15¼:17¼)in/30(37:39:44)cm from cast on edge, ending with a p row.

Shape neck

Next row K16(18:20:22) sts, turn and work on these sts for first side of neck shaping.

Bind off 4 sts at beg of next row.

Dec one st at neck edge on every foll alt row until 8(10:12:13) sts rem.

Cont without further shaping until front measures same as Back to shoulder, ending at side edge.

Shape shoulder

Bind off.

With right side facing, slip center 10(12:14:14) sts onto a holder, rejoin yarn to rem sts, k to end.

Complete to match first side, reversing shaping.

Sleeves

With US 2(2¾mm) needles cast on 32(36:40:44) sts.

K 5 rows.

Change to US 3(3¼mm) needles.

Beg with a k row, work in st st.

Inc one st at each end of the 5th and every foll 6th row until there are 50(56:62:68) sts.

Cont straight until sleeve measures 6¼(8½:9½:10¼)in/ 18(22:24:26)cm from cast on edge, ending with a p row.

Shape top

Bind off 4 sts at beg of next 2 rows.

Dec one st at each end of the next 5 rows, then every 3(4:5:6) foll alt rows. Dec one st at each end of every row until 8(10:12:14) sts rem.

Bind off.

Neckband

Join shoulder seams.

With right side facing and US 2(2¾mm) circular needle, slip 8(8:10:10) sts from left back holder onto needle, pick up and k9(10:9:10) sts up left back neck to shoulder, 15(16:20:20) sts down left front neck, k across 10(12:14:14) sts from front neck holder, pick up and k15(16:20:20) sts up right front neck to shoulder, 9(10:9:10) sts down right back neck, then k across 8(8:10:10) sts on right back neck holder. 74(80:92:94) sts.

Work backwards and forwards in rows.

K 3 rows.

Eyelet row (right side) K3(6:2:3), * k2tog, yf, k3; rep from * to last 6(9:5:6) sts, k2tog, yf, k4(7:3:4).

K 2 rows.

Bind off.

Edging

With US 3(3¼mm) needles cast on 4 sts.

K 1 row.

1st row (right side) K2, yf, k2.

2nd, 4th and 6th rows K to end.

3rd row K3, yf, k2.

5th row K2, yf, k2tog, yf, k2.

7th row K3, yf, k2tog, yf, k2.

8th row Bind off 4 sts, k to end.

These 8 rows form the patt.

Work in patt until edging, when slightly stretched, fits along lower edge of dress, ending with an 8th patt row.

Bind off.

Finish

Sew on sleeves. Join side and sleeve seams. Make button loop on neckband of left back. Sew on button. Sew edging to hem of dress, joining cast on and bound off edges together. Cut ribbon in half. Stitch one end of each length securely to the inside of back neckband. Thread ribbon through eyelets and tie at center front.

embroidered jacket

Folkloric-style embroidery is used to embellish this jacket. If you would prefer a simpler look, you could decorate the collar and cuffs only.

Measurements

To fit ages	6-12	12-18	mths

Actual measurements

Chest	24	27½	in
	61	70	cm

Length to shoulder

	11	13	in
	28	33	cm

Sleeve length (with cuff turned back)

	8	9	in
	20	23	cm

Materials

4(5) 50g/2oz balls of Debbie Bliss merino double knitting.
Small amounts of wool in Bright Blue, Pale Blue, Cream, Red, Fuchsia, Bright Pink, Dark Green, Mid Green, Lilac and Stone for embroidery.
Pair each of US 3(3¼mm) and US 6 (4mm) knitting needles.
5(6) buttons.

Gauge

22 sts and 30 rows to 4in/10cm square over st st using US 6(4mm) needles.

Abbreviations See page 7.

Back and Fronts

Worked in one piece to armholes.
With US 3(3¼mm) needles cast on 143(159) sts.
K 2 rows.
Buttonhole row (right side) K1, k2tog, yf, k to end.
K 2 rows.
Change to US 6(4mm) needles.
1st row K to end.
2nd row K5, p to last 5 sts, k5.
These 2 rows set the st st with garter st borders.
Work 4(5) more buttonholes from this point to neck shaping, with 2in/5cm between each.
Cont straight until work measures 6(7)in/15(18)cm from cast on edge, ending with a wrong side row.

Divide for Back and Fronts

Next row K37(41), leave these sts on a holder for right front, k next 69(77), leave these sts on a holder for back, k to end.

Left Front

Work straight on last set of 37(41) sts until front measures 9(11)in/23(28)cm from cast on edge, ending at neck edge.

Shape neck

Next row Bind off 3 sts, k next st, p3, place last 5 sts on a safety pin, p to end.
Dec one st at neck edge on every row until 20(22) sts rem.
Cont straight until work measures 11(13)in/28(33)cm from cast on edge, ending at armhole edge.

Shape shoulder

Bind off 10(11) sts at beg of next row.
Work 1 row.
Bind off rem 10(11) sts.

Back

With wrong side facing, rejoin yarn to next st, p69(77) sts. Cont straight until work measures same as Left Front to shoulder, ending with a p row.

Shape shoulders

Bind off 10(11) sts at beg of next 4 rows.

Leave rem 29(33) sts on a spare needle.

Right Front

With wrong side facing, rejoin yarn to next st, p to to last 5 sts, k5.

Work to match Left Front, working rem 2 buttonholes and reversing all shapings.

Sleeves

With US 6(4mm) needles cast on 38(42) sts.

K 5 rows.

Beg with a k row, work in st st until work measures 1½in/4cm from cast on edge, ending with a p row.

K 4 rows.

Change to US 3(3¼mm) needles.

Beg with a p row, work in st st for 2in/5cm.

Change to US 6(4mm) needles.

Cont in st st, inc one st at each end of the next and every foll 3rd row until there are 58(64) sts.

Cont straight until sleeve measures 10¼(11½)in/26(29)cm from cast on edge, ending with a p row. Bind off.

Collar

Join shoulder seams.

With right side facing and using US 6(4mm) needles, slip 5 sts from right front safety pin onto a needle, pick up and k18 sts up right front neck, k29(33) sts across back neck, pick up and k18 sts down left side of front neck, k5 sts from safety pin. 75(79) sts.

Next row K to end.

Next row K5, p to last 5 sts, k5.

Rep the last 2 rows 8 times more.

K 4 rows. Bind off.

Finish

Join sleeve seams reversing seam on cuff. Sew in sleeves. Sew on buttons.

To embroider

Using all the contrast shades, embroider flowers and leaves in satin stitch, stem stitch, chain stitch and French knots, see diagrams below and on following page. See page 105 for stitch instructions.

Key

■	Bright Blue	■	Bright Punk
■	Pale Blue	■	Dark Green
□	Cream	■	Mid Green
■	Red	■	Lilac
■	Fuchsia	□	Stone

COLLAR EMBROIDERY
(reverse for other collar point)

CUFF EMBROIDERY

Key

■ Bright Blue   ■ Bright Punk
■ Pale Blue   ■ Dark Green
☐ Cream   ■ Mid Green
■ Red   ■ Lilac
■ Fuchsia   ■ Stone

satin stitch

stem stitch
(all stems and leaf veins)

French knots

satin stitch

satin stitch
(all flower petals
and leaves)

LEFT FRONT | BACK

LEFT FRONT EMBROIDERY
(reverse for RIGHT FRONT)

FRONT NECK EMBROIDERY

Baby's Kaftan
(page 102)

Key

■ Fuchsia
■ Red
■ Turquoise
□ Yellow
■ Olive

French knots

satin stitch

chain stitch

CUFF EMBROIDERY

French knots

satin stitch

satin stitch

chain stitch

BACK NECK EMBROIDERY

chain stitch

satin stitch

chain stitch

chain stitch

TOE OF RIGHT SHOE
(reverse for LEFT SHOE)

chain stitch

satin stitch

stem stitch

chain stitch

chain stitch

satin stitch

stem stitch

satin stitch

French knot

satin stitch

stem stitch

satin stitch

Embroidered Shoes
(page 116)

Key

■ Red
□ Mauve
■ Fuschia
■ Khaki
□ Yellow
■ Duckegg blue
■ Turquoise

embroidery diagrams **101**

baby's kaftan

Knitted in a cotton mix, this simple V-neck top is decorated with rich floral embroidery to create an Eastern effect.

Measurements

To fit ages

3-6	6-9	9-12	mths

Actual measurements

Chest

19¾	21¼	22¾	in
50	54	58	cm

Length to shoulder

11	11¾	12½	in
28	30	32	cm

Sleeve seam

6¼	6¾	7	in
16	17	18	cm

Materials

3(4:4) 50g/2oz balls of Debbie Bliss wool/cotton in Main shade (M) and small amounts of wool/cotton in Fuchsia, Red, Turquoise, Yellow and Olive for embroidery.
Pair each of US 2-3(3mm) and US 3(3¼mm) knitting needles.

Gauge

25 sts and 34 rows to 4in/10cm square over st st using US 3(3¼mm) needles.

Abbreviations See page 7.

Back

With US 2-3(3mm) needles cast on 64(68:72) sts.
K 3 rows.
Change to US 3(3¼mm) needles.
Next row (wrong side) K2, p to last 2 sts, k2.
K 1 row.
Rep the last 2 rows twice more.
Beg with a p row, work in st st until back measures 6¼(6¾:7)in/16(17:18)cm, ending with a p row.

Shape armholes
Bind off 3 sts at beg of next 2 rows.
Dec one st at each end of next and 3(3:4) foll alt rows. 50(54:56) sts.
Work until back measures 10¼(11:11¾)in/26(28:30)cm, ending with a p row.

Shape neck
Next row K16(17:18), turn and leave rem sts on a holder.
Dec one st at neck edge of next 4 rows.
P 1 row.

Shape shoulder
Bind off 6(6:7) sts at beg of next row.
P 1 row.
Bind off rem 6(7:7) sts.
With right side facing, slip center 18(20:20) sts onto a holder, rejoin yarn to rem 16(17:18) sts, k to end.
Complete to match first side of neck shaping.

Front

Work as given for Back until front measures 7½(7¾:8¼)in/ 19(20:21)cm from cast on edge, ending with a p row.

Shape front opening

Next row K24(26:27) sts, turn and work on these sts for the first side of front neck.

Cont straight until front measures 9¾(10¾:11½)in/25(27:29)cm, ending with a k row.

Shape neck

Bind off 6(7:7) sts at the beg of next row.

Dec one st at neck edge on next 6 rows. 12(13:14) sts.

Cont until front measures same as Back to shoulder, ending at side edge.

Shape shoulder

Bind off 6(6:7) sts at beg of next row.

P 1 row.

Bind off rem 6(7:7) sts.

With right side facing, rejoin yarn, bind off center 2 sts, k to end.

Complete to match first side of neck shaping.

Sleeves

With US 2-3(3mm) needles cast on 43(43:47) sts.

K 3 rows.

Change to US 3(3¼mm) needles.

Beg with a k row, work in st st, inc one st at each end of next and every foll 5th row until there are 59(65:71) sts.

Cont straight until sleeve measures 6¼(6¾:7)in/16(17:18)cm from cast on edge, ending with a p row.

Shape top

Bind off 3 sts at beg of next 2 rows.

Dec one st at each end of next and 3(3:4) foll alt rows.

Bind off rem 45(51:55) sts.

Neckband

Join right shoulder seam.

With right side facing and US 3(3¼mm) needles, pick up and k15(16:16) sts down left front neck, pick up and k20(22:24) sts down left front opening, k2 center front sts, pick up and k20(22:24) sts up right front opening, pick up and k15(16:16) sts up right front neck, k5 sts down right back neck, k across 18(20:20) sts from back neck holder, pick up and k5 sts up left back neck. 100(108:112) sts.

Bind off.

Finish

Join left shoulder and neckband seam. Sew sleeves into armholes. Join side and sleeve seams.

Embroidery

Work embroidery around neck and sleeve edges in colors and stitches as given in diagrams on page 101. See below for stitch instructions.

Embroidery stitches

1 Stem stitch Bring the needle and the thread through the knitting, then insert the needle as shown, at a slight angle. Pull the needle through. Continue making short, slightly angled stitches in this way from left the right.

2 French knots Bring the needle and thread through. Wind the thread around the needle twice. Keeping the thread tautly wrapped around the needle, reinsert the needle very near where the thread first emerged and take it through to the back of the knitting.

3 Satin stitch Bring the needle and thread through. Then work parallel stitches close together. The stitches can be made straight across or at an angle depending on the effect desired. Do not pull the thread too tightly or the knitting will become distorted.

4 Chain stitch Bring the needle and thread through. Then reinsert the needle where the thread first emerged and bring it out a short distance away, making sure that it comes out above the thread to form a loop. Continue making loops in the same way.

sheep dress and shoes

This smock-style dress has a trellis-patterned yoke and sheep grazing around the hem. There is a picot edge for a delicate lace effect.

Measurements

Dress: To fit ages

6-9	9-12	12-24	mths

Actual measurements

Chest

22¾	25¼	27½	in
58	64	70	cm

Length to shoulder

13¾	15½	17	in
35	39	43	cm

Sleeve length

6¼	8½	9½	in
16	22	24	cm

Shoes: To fit ages

6-9	9-12	mths

Materials

Dress: 7(8:10) 50g/2oz balls of Debbie Bliss wool/cotton in Main shade (M). One 50g/2oz ball each in Black and White.
Pair each of US 2-3(3 mm) and US 3(3¼mm) knitting needles.
Cable needle.
Shoes: One 50g/2oz ball of Debbie Bliss wool/cotton in Main shade (M) and small amount of Black and White.
Pair each of US 2(2¾mm) and US 2-3(3mm) knitting needles.
Cable needle.
2 small buttons.

Gauge

25 sts and 34 rows to 4in/10cm square over st st using US 3 (3¼mm) needles.

Abbreviations

C2B = cross 2 back, slip next st onto cable needle and leave at back of work, k1, then k1 from cable needle.
C2F = cross 2 front, slip next st onto cable needle and leave at front of work, k1, then k1 from cable needle.
Cr2L = cross 2 left, slip next st onto cable needle and leave at front of work, p1, then k1 from cable needle.
Cr2R = cross 2 right, slip next st onto cable needle and leave at back of work, k1, then p1 from cable needle.
See also page 7.

Note Read charts from right to left on right side rows and from left to right on wrong side rows. When working color motifs, use separate lengths of contrast yarn for each colored area and twist yarns together on wrong side at joins to avoid holes.

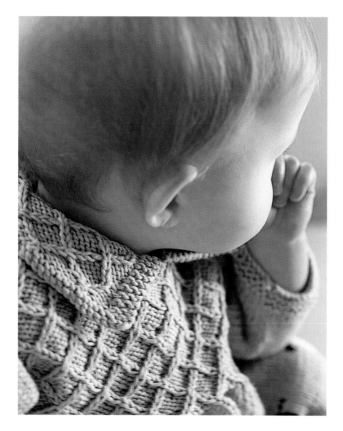

DRESS

Back

With US 3(3¼mm) needles and M, cast on 117(127:137) sts.

Beg with a k row, work 8 rows in st st. Cont in patt.

1st row K5(8:11)M, * work across 1st row of Chart A, k8(9:10)M; rep from * to last 20(23:26) sts, work across 1st row of Chart A, k5(8:11)M.

2nd row P5(8:11)M, * work across 2nd row of Chart A, p8(9:10)M; rep from * to last 20(23:26) sts, work across 2nd row of Chart A, p5(8:11)M.

Cont in patt to end of Chart A.

Work in st st until back measures 8½(9¾:11)in/22(25:28)cm from cast on edge, ending with a right side row.

Shape armholes

Bind off 5 sts at beg of next 2 rows. 107(117:127) sts.

Dec row P2(5:7), [p2tog, p2tog, p1] 20(21:22) times, p2tog, p3(5:8). 66(74:82) sts.

Work in patt as follows:

1st row (right side) P4, [C2F, p6] to last 6 sts, C2F, p4.

2nd row K3, [Cr2L, Cr2R, k4] to last 7 sts, Cr2L, Cr2R, k3.

3rd row P2, [Cr2R, p2, Cr2L, p2] to end.

4th row K1, [Cr2L, k4, Cr2R] to last st, k1.

5th row P1, k1, [p6, C2B] to last 8 sts, p6, k1, p1.

6th row K1, [Cr2R, k4, Cr2L] to last st, k1.

7th row P2, [Cr2L, p2, Cr2R, p2] to end.

8th row K3, [Cr2R, Cr2L, k4] to last 7 sts, Cr2R, Cr2L, k3.

These 8 rows form the yoke patt.

Cont in patt until back measures 13¾(15½:17)in/35(39:43)cm from beg, ending with a wrong side row.

Shape neck and shoulders

Next row Patt 23(26:29), bind off next 20(22:24) sts, patt to end.

Work on last set of 23(26:29) sts for first side of back neck.

** Bind off 6(7:8) sts at beg of next row and 3 sts at beg of foll row.

Rep the last 2 rows once more.

Bind off rem 5(6:7) sts. **

With wrong side facing, rejoin yarn to rem sts and patt to end.

Complete as given for first side from ** to **.

Chart A

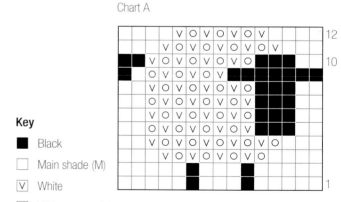

Key

■ Black

☐ Main shade (M)

Ⅴ White

○ White – p on right side rows, k on wrong side rows

Front

Work as given for Back until front measures 11¾(13½:15)in/ 30(34:38)cm from cast on edge, ending with a wrong side row.

Shape neck

Next row Patt 28(31:34), turn and work on these sts for first side of front neck.

Dec one st at neck edge on every row until 17(20:23) sts rem. Work straight until front matches Back to shoulder shaping, ending at armhole edge.

Shape shoulder

Bind off 6(7:8) sts at beg of next and foll alt row.

Work 1 row.

Bind off rem 5(6:7) sts.

With right side facing, rejoin yarn to rem sts, bind off center 10(12:14) sts, patt to end.

Complete to match first side of neck shaping.

Sleeves

With US 2-3(3mm) needles and M, cast on 36(39:42) sts. K 5 rows.

Inc row K3, * m1, k3; rep from * to end. 47(51:55) sts. Change to US 3(3¼mm) needles.

Beg with a k row, work in st st, inc one st at each end of the 5th and every foll 4th row until there are 69(77:83) sts. Cont straight until sleeve measures 7(9½:10)in/18(24:26)cm from cast on edge, ending with a wrong side row. Bind off.

Collar

With US 3(3¼mm) needles and M, cast on 96(104:112) sts. K 3 rows.

Work in patt as follows:

1st row (right side) K3, p4, [C2F, p6] to last 9 sts, C2F, p4, k3.
2nd row K6, [Cr2L, Cr2R, k4] to last 10 sts, Cr2L, Cr2R, k6.
3rd row K3, p2, [Cr2R, p2, Cr2L, p2] to last 3 sts, k3.
4th row K4, [Cr2L, k4, Cr2R] to last 4 sts, k4.
5th row K3, p1, k1, [p6, C2B] to last 11 sts, p6, k1, p1, k3.
6th row K4, [Cr2R, k4, Cr2L] to last 4 sts, k4.

7th row K3, p2, [Cr2L, p2, Cr2R, p2] to last 3 sts, k3.
8th row K6, [Cr2R, Cr2L, k4] to last 10 sts, Cr2R, Cr2L, k6.
Work a further 12 rows in patt.
Bind off 9 sts at beg of next 2 rows.
Bind off 8(9:10) sts at beg of next 6 rows.
Bind off rem 30(32:34) sts.

Finish

Join shoulder seams. Sew sleeves into armholes, sewing row ends of last ¾in/2cm to sts bound off at underarm. Join side and sleeve seams. Sew shaped edge of collar to neck edge.

Edging

With right side facing, US 2-3(3mm) needles and White, work along cast on edges of back and front, picking up and casting off at the same time as follows:

Pick up and k2 sts, bind off one st, * slip st used in casting off back onto left-hand needle, cast on 2 sts, bind off 2 sts, [pick up and k one st, bind off one st] 4 times, rep from * to end. Fasten off.

SHOES
Right Shoe

With US 2-3(3 mm) needles and M, cast on 34(40) sts.
K 1 row.

1st row K1, yf, k15(18), [yf, k1] twice, yf, k15(18), yf, k1.

2nd and 4 foll alt rows K to end, working k1 tbl into yf of previous row.

3rd row K2, yf, k15(18), yf, k2, yf, k3, yf, k15(18), yf, k2.

5th row K3, yf, k15(18), [yf, k4] twice, yf, k15(18), yf, k3.

7th row K4, yf, k15(18), yf, k5, yf, k6, yf, k15(18), yf, k4.

9th row K5, yf, k15(18), [yf, k7] twice, yf, k15(18), yf, k5.

11th row K2, [yf, k4] 7 times, [yf, k3] 0(2) times, [yf, k4] 7 times, yf, k1. 74(82) sts.

12th row (wrong side) Working k1 tbl into yf of previous row, work as follows: k4, [p2, k6] to last 6 sts, p2, k4.

Beg with a 1st patt row, work 9 rows in yoke patt as given for Back of dress.

Next row (wrong side) K4, [p2tog, k6] to last 6 sts, p2tog, k4. 65(72) sts.

Shape instep

1st size only

1st row K38, skpo, turn.

2nd size only

1st row K35, k2tog, k5, turn.

Both sizes

2nd row Sl 1, p11, p2tog, turn.

3rd row Sl 1, k11, skpo, turn.

4th row Sl 1, p11, p2tog, turn.

5th row Sl 1, k acoss 1st row of Chart B, skpo, turn.

6th row Sl 1, p across 2nd row of Chart B, skpo, turn.

7th to 12th rows Rep 5th and 6th rows 3 times, working 3rd to 8th rows of Chart B.

Rep 3rd and 4th rows 2(3) times more.

Next row Sl 1, k to end.

Bind off, decreasing one st at each corner.

Join sole and back seam.

With right side facing, US 2-3(3mm) needles and beginning and ending 8 sts at either side of back seam, pick up and

k17 sts along heel edge. K 1 row. **

Next row Cast on 3 sts, k to end, turn and cast on 19 sts.
K 1 row.

Buttonhole row K35, yf, k2tog, k2.
K 2 rows. Bind off.

Edging

With right side facing, US 2(2¾mm) needles and White, work around top edge of shoe and pick up and bind off at the same time as follows: Pick up and k2 sts, bind off one st, * slip st used in casting off back onto left-hand needle, cast on 2 sts, bind off 2 sts, [pick up and k one st, bind off one st] 4 times, rep from * to end. Fasten off. Sew on button.

Left Shoe

Work as given for Right Shoe to **, working from Chart C instead of Chart B.

Next row Cast on 19 sts, k to end, turn and cast on 3 sts.
K 1 row.

Buttonhole row K2, k2tog, yf, k to end.
K 2 rows. Bind off.

Edging

With right side facing, US 2(2¾mm) needles and White, work around top edge of shoe and pick up and bind off at the same time as follows: Pick up and k2 sts, bind off one st, * slip st used in casting off back onto left-hand needle, cast on 2 sts, bind off 2 sts, [pick up and k one st, bind off one st] 4 times, rep from * to end. Fasten off. Sew on button.

Chart B   Chart C

Key

■ Black   ☑ White

☐ Main shade (M)   ◙ White – p on right side rows, k on wrong side rows

cardigan with frilled sleeves

The flounce on the sleeves of this simple stockinette stitch cardigan gives it a party feel. It is knitted in a soft wool and cotton mix.

Measurements
To fit ages
| 9-12 | 12-18 | 24-36 | mths |

Actual measurements
Chest
| 24½ | 27½ | 30 | in |
| 62 | 70 | 76 | cm |

Length to shoulder
| 11 | 12½ | 14¼ | in |
| 28 | 32 | 36 | cm |

Sleeve length (including frill)
| 6 | 6¾ | 7½ | in |
| 15 | 17 | 19 | cm |

Materials
4(4:5) 50g/2oz balls of Debbie Bliss wool/cotton.
Pair each of US 2(2¾mm), US 3 (3¼mm) and US 5(3¾mm) knitting needles.
Long US 3(3¼mm) circular knitting needle.
2 stitch holders.
6(6:7) buttons.

Gauge
25 sts and 34 rows to 4in/10cm square over st st using US 3 (3¼mm) needles.

Abbreviations See page 7.

Back and Fronts
Worked in one piece to armholes.
With US 2(2¾mm) needles cast on 156(176:192) sts.
K 4 rows.
Change to US 3(3¼mm) needles.
Beg with a k row, work in st st until work measures 6¼(7½:8¾)in/16(19:22)cm from cast on edge, ending with a p row.

Divide for Back and Fronts
Next row K39(44:48) sts, leave these sts on a holder for right front, k next 78(88:96) sts, leave these sts on a holder for back, k to end.

Left Front
Work straight on last set of 39(44:48) sts until front measures 8(9:10¼)in/20(23:26)cm from cast on edge, ending with a p row.

Shape neck
Next row K to last 4 sts, k2tog, k2.
Next row P2, p2tog, p to end.
Dec one st at neck edge on every row until 20(24:27) sts rem.
Work straight until front measures 11(12½:14¼)in/ 28(32:36)cm from cast on edge, ending with a p row.

Shape shoulder
Bind off 10(12:13) sts beg of next row.
P 1 row.
Bind off rem 10(12:14) sts.

Back
With wrong side facing, rejoin yarn to next st on holder, p78(88:96) sts, turn.
Work on this set of sts only until back measures same

as Left Front to shoulder shaping, ending with a p row.

Shape shoulder

Bind off 10(12:13) sts at beg of next 2 rows.

Bind off 10(12:14) sts at beg of foll 2 rows.

Bind off rem 38(40:42) sts.

Right Front

With wrong side facing, rejoin yarn to rem sts on holder, p to end.

Cont in st st until work measures 8(9:10¼)in/20(23:26)cm from cast on edge, ending with a p row.

Shape neck

Next row K2, skpo, k to end.

Next row P to last 4 sts, p2togtbl, p2.

Complete to match left front.

Sleeves

With US 2(2¾mm) needles, cast on 42(46:52) sts.

K 2 rows.

Change to US 3(3¼mm) needles.

Beg with a k row, work in st st, inc one st at each end of every foll 4th(5th:5th) row until there are 61(66:72) sts.

Cont straight until sleeve measures 5¼(6¼:7)in/14(16:18)cm from cast on edge, ending with a p row.

Bind off.

Front and Neck Bands

Join shoulder seams.

With right side facing and US 3(3¼mm) circular needle, pick up and k49(57:65) sts up right front edge to beg of neck shaping, 27(29:33) sts up right front neck to shoulder seam, 28(30:32) sts across back neck edge, 27(29:33) sts down left front neck to beg of neck shaping and 49(57:65) sts down left front to cast on edge. 180(202:228) sts.

Next row K to end.

Next row K1(2:2), k2tog, yf, [k7(8:8), k2tog, yf] 5(5:6) times, k to end.

Next row K to end.

Bind off.

Sleeve Edgings

With right side facing and US 3(3¼mm) needles, pick up and k42(46:52) sts along lower edge of sleeve.

Next row P1, [inc in next st] 40(44:50) times, p1.

Beg with a k row, work 6 rows in st st.

Change to US 5(3¾mm) needles.

Work a further 4 rows.

Bind off.

Finish

Join sleeve seams. Sew sleeves into armholes.

Sew on buttons.

fair isle bag

The perfect baby accessory to decorate the nursery, this pretty baby bag has a beaded picot edge.

Measurements
Approximately 7 x 8in/17 x 20cm.

Materials
One 50g/2oz ball of Debbie Bliss wool/cotton in each of Main shade Pale Pink (M), Brown, Dark Aqua, Cream and Dark Red, and small amount of Yellow.
Pair of US 3(3¼mm) knitting needles.
29 small knitting beads.

Gauge
25 sts and 34 rows to 4in/10cm square over st st using US 3(3¼mm) needles.

Abbreviations See page 7.

Note Read chart from right to left on right side rows and from left to right on wrong side rows. When working in patt, strand yarn not in use loosely across wrong side to keep fabric elastic.

To make

Thread the beads onto M and with US 3(3¼mm) needles, work a beaded picot cast on edge as follows: [Cast on 5 sts, k1, bring yarn and 1 bead forward to the front of the work, slip 1 st purlwise, then holding bead to the front, take yarn back and pass k st over sl st, k1, bind off 1, place rem st on right-hand needle back onto left-hand needle] 29 times, cast on 2 sts. 89 sts.

Beg with a k row, work in st st.

Work 6 rows.

Dec row K9, [k2tog, k21] 3 times, k2tog, k9. 85 sts.

P 1 row.

Eyelet row K3, [k2tog, yf, k5] 11 times, k2tog, yf, k3.

Work 3 rows.

Inc row K9, [m1, k22] 3 times, m1, k10. 89 sts.

Work 3 rows.

Beg with a k row, cont in st st and work 37 rows from Chart, working the edge st at beg of k rows and the end of p rows and repeating the 8 patt sts across the row.

Cont in Brown only.

P 1 row.

Shape base

Next row (right side) K1, [k2tog, k6] to end. 78 sts.

P 1 row.

Next row K1, [k2tog, k5] to end. 67 sts.

P 1 row.

Cont to decrease in this way working one less st between decreases on every alt row until 12 sts rem.

Break yarn, thread through sts, pull up and secure.

Join seam.

Drawstrings (make 2)

With Brown, make two 20in/51cm long narrow plaits. Thread through the eyelets, the first plait starting and ending either side of the seam, the second directly opposite. Tie the plait ends together and pull up to close the bag.

Key

- ▢ Pale Pink (M)
- ◼ Brown
- ▨ Dark Aqua
- ▢ Cream
- ◼ Dark Red
- ▨ Yellow

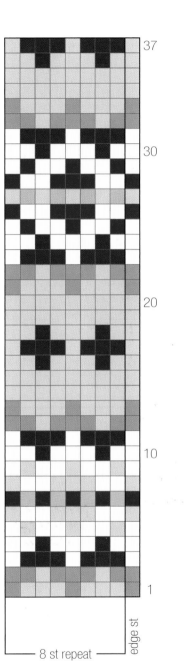

37

30

20

10

1

edge st

8 st repeat

embroidered shoes

Inspired by Chinese slippers, these knitted shoes are embellished with sumptuous flowers and leaves.

Measurements

To fit age   6-12   mths

Materials

One 50g/2oz ball of Debbie Bliss wool/cotton in Main shade (M) and small amounts of Red, Mauve, Fuchsia, Khaki, Yellow, Duckegg Blue and Turquoise for embroidery.
Pair of US 3(3¼mm) knitting needles.

Gauge

30 sts and 52 rows to 4in/10cm square over garter st (k every row) using US 3(3¼mm) needles.

Abbreviations See page 7.

To make

With US 3(3¼mm) needles and M, cast on 13 sts for top. K 20 rows. Leave sts on a holder.

With US 3(3¼mm) needles and M, cast on 17 sts, with right side facing, pick up and k14 sts along right edge of top, k13 sts from holder, pick up and k14 sts along left edge of top, turn and cast on 17 sts. 75 sts.

K 11 rows.

Shape sole

1st row Sl 1, k32, k2tog, k5, k2tog, k to end.

2nd row Sl 1, k31, k2tog, k5, k2tog, k to end.

3rd row Sl 1, k2, k2tog, k24, k2tog, k3, k3tog, k3, k2tog, k24, k2tog, k3.

4th and 5th rows Sl 1, k to end.

6th row K2tog, [k3, k2tog, k22, k2tog] twice, k3, k2tog.

7th and 8th rows Sl 1, k to end.

9th row K2tog, k2, k2tog, k18, [k2tog, k1] 4 times, k17, k2tog, k2, k2tog.

10th row Sl 1, k to end.

11th row Sl 1, [k2tog, k1] 3 times, k10, [k2tog, k1] 4 times, k10, [k2tog, k1] 3 times. 41 sts. Bind off.

Finish

Join back and sole seam.

To embroider

Using all the contrast shades, embroider flowers and leaves in satin stitch, stem stitch, chain stitch, backstitch, and French knots on right shoe (see diagram on page 101), then work a mirror image on the left shoe. See page 105 for stitch instructions.

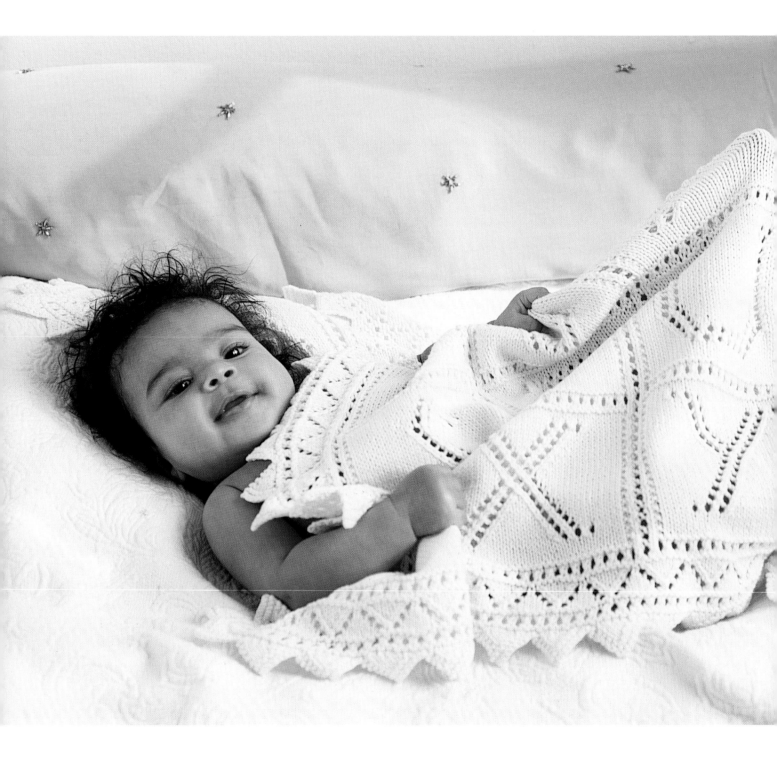

alphabet blanket

The alphabet is picked out in delicate lace stitches in this intricately worked blanket designed for a cherished baby. It is enhanced by a pretty decorative edging.

Measurements
Approximately 35½ x 35½in/90 x 90cm.

Materials
Eleven 50g/2oz balls of Debbie Bliss wool/cotton.
Pair each of long US 2(2¾mm) and US 3(3¼mm) knitting needles or circular needles.

Gauge
25 sts and 34 rows to 4in/10cm square over st st using US 3(3¼mm) needles.

Abbreviations See page 7.

Chart note Read chart from right to left on right side rows and from left to right on wrong side rows.

Note If working on circular needles, work in rows not rounds.
For a completely flat finish to the edging, use a smooth contrast color yarn to cast on and, when completed, do not bind off. Leave sts on the needle and cont to work top border on these sts. To work the lower border, undo the cast on row, placing the loops on a US 3(3¼mm) circular or long needle.

To make
Using US 3(3¼mm) long or circular needle, loosely cast on 187 sts.
Beg with 1st row, work in patt from Alphabet Blocks Chart on pages 120–123. Bind off (see Note).

Top Border
With right side facing and US 3(3¼mm) long or circular needle, pick up and k187 sts. P 1 row. Omit the last 2 rows if sts have been left on needle. Work 12 rows of Border Chart. 199 sts.
Transfer sts to US 2(2¾mm) long or circular needle.

Triangle edging
1st row (right side) P1, turn. **2nd row** P1. **3rd row** P2, turn. **4th row** P2. **5th row** P2, k1, turn. **6th row** P3. **7th row** P2, k2, turn. **8th row** P4. **9th row** P2, k3, turn. **10th row** P5. **11th row** P2, k4, turn. **12th row** P6. **13th row** P7, turn. **14th row** P7. **15th row** Bind off 8 sts purlwise, one st on right needle, turn.
Rep 2nd to 15th rows, until 15th row of last triangle, then bind off rem 7 sts.

Lower Border
With right side facing and US 3(3¼mm) long or circular needle, pick up and k187 sts. P 1 row.
Omit the last 2 rows if cast on sts have been undone.
Work 12 rows of Border Chart. 199 sts.
Transfer sts to US 2(2¾mm) long or circular needle and work triangle edging as given for Top Border.

Side Borders
With right side facing and US 3(3¼mm) long or circular needle, pick up and k227 sts along right side edge. Work 12 rows of Border Chart. 239 sts.
Transfer sts onto a US 2(2¾mm) long or circular needle and work triangle edging as given for Top Border.
Work border along left side as given for right side.

Finish
Join corner seams.

Note Read each chart row all the way across this page and the page opposite. Chart continues on next two pages.

130

121

111

101

91

81

71

61

51

41

31

21

11

1

Key

☐ k on right side rows, p on wrong side rows

• p on right side rows

╱ k2tog on right side rows, p2tog on wrong side rows

╲ skpo

○ yarn over needle to make a stitch

◢ k3tog

◣ slip 1, k2tog, psso

Border Chart

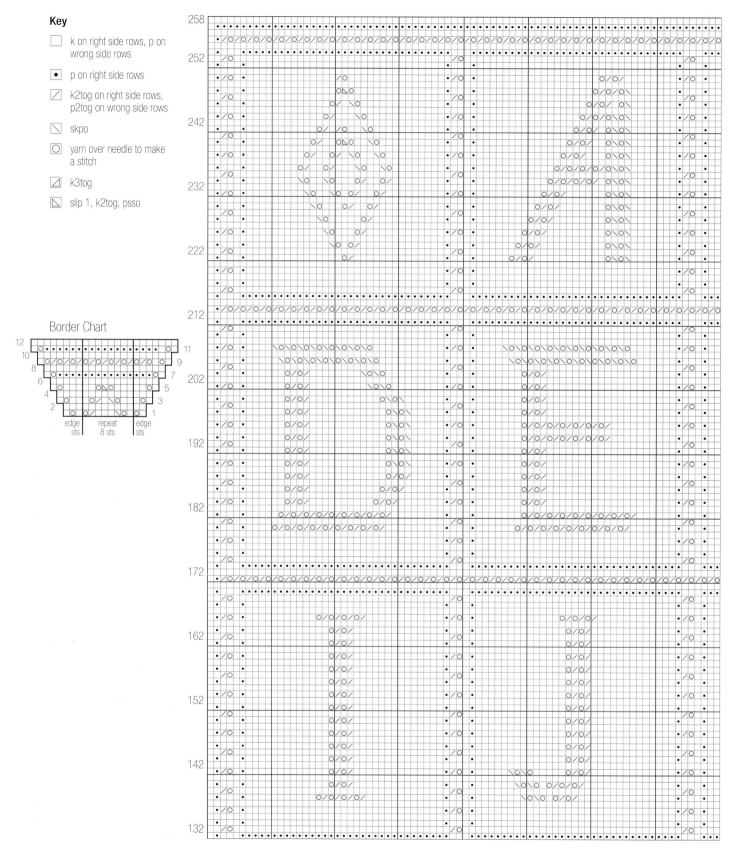

257
251
241
231
221
211
201
191
181
171
161
151
141
131

Note This chart starts on pages 120 and 121. Again, read each chart row across this page and the page opposite.

alphabet blanket **123**

the finishing touch

These simple garter stitch shoes are enhanced by introducing different elements to decorate the edge. As alternatives, you could pick up stitches around the edge and use the picot bind off from the sheep dress and shoes, embroider on simple lazy daisy stitches, or sew on tiny rose buds. I have used velvet piping, beads and fine ribbon, but you will find other ways to bring your own original style to this simple shoe pattern.

garter stitch shoes

Measurements

To fit ages   3-6   9-12   12-18   mths

Materials

One 50g/2oz ball of Debbie Bliss baby cashmerino.
Pair of US 2(2³⁄₄mm) knitting needles.
Beaded shoes: Approximately 250 small beads.
Ribbon shoes: 20in/50cm of narrow ribbon.
Piped edge shoes: 20in/50cm narrow velvet piping.

Gauge

28 sts and 60 rows to 4in/10cm square over garter st (k every row) using US 2(2³⁄₄mm) needles.

Abbreviations See page 7.

Note For safety reasons, make sure that beads are stitched on securely.

To make

With US 2(2¾mm) needles, cast on 18(22:26) sts.

K 1 row.

Work in garter st and inc one st at each end of next and every foll alt row until there are 32(38:44) sts.

Dec one st at each end of next and every foll alt row until 18(22:26) sts rem.

Shape heel

Next row Cast on 7(8:9) sts, k these 7(8:9) sts, then k to end. 25(30:35) sts.

K 1 row.

Inc one st at end of next row and 5(6:7) foll alt rows. 31(37:43) sts.

K 1 row.

Next row Bind off 18(20:22) sts, k to last st, inc in last st. 14(18:22) sts.

K 14(18:22) rows.

Next row K2tog, k to end.

Next row Cast on 18(20:22) sts, k these 18(20:22) sts, then k to end. 31(37:43) sts.

Dec one st at beg of next and 5(6:7) foll alt rows. 25(30:35) sts.

K 1 row.

Bind off.

Finish

Join back heel seam. Join upper to sole all around easing in fullness at toes. Turn through to right side.

Beaded shoes–stitch small beads around the edge of each shoe.

Ribbon shoes–use a large eyed blunt needle to thread narrow ribbon around the edge of each shoe, beg and ending ¼in/5mm to either side of center front. Tie in a bow.

Piped edge shoes–folding the cut ends under, stitch piping around the edge of each shoe.

Suppliers of Debbie Bliss Yarn

See page 9 for descriptions of Debbie Bliss yarns. For suppliers, please contact one of the following distributors:

USA Knitting Fever Inc,
35 Debevoise Avenue, Roosevelt, NY 11575.
Tel: (516) 546-3600. Fax: (516) 546-6871.
www.knittingfever.com

UK Designer Yarns Ltd,
1 Tivoli Place, Ilkley, West Yorkshire LS29 8SU.
Tel: (01943) 604 123. Fax: (01943) 600 320.
tivolipl@aol.com

Canada Diamond Yarns Ltd,
155 Martin Ross Avenue, Unit 3, Toronto, Ontario M3J 2L9.
Tel: (416) 736-6111. Fax: (416) 736-6112.
www.diamondyarn.com

Australia Sunspun Inspirations,
185 Canterbury Road, Canterbury, VIC 3126.
Tel: 03 9830 1609. Fax: 03 9888 5658.

Japan Eisaku Noro & Co Ltd,
55 Shimoda Ohibino Azaichou,
Ichinomita Aichi, 491 0105.
Tel: +81 52 203 5100. Fax: +81 52 203 5077.

Germany Klaus Koch,
Pontinusweg 7, D-50859 Köln.
Tel: +49 0170 5803 316. Fax: +49 02234 77573.
www.debbiebliss.de

France Elle Tricote,
8 Rue de Coq (Petite France), 67000 Strasbourg.
Tel: 0388 23 03 13. Fax: 0388 23 01 69.
www.elletricote.com

Belgium and Netherlands Pavan,
Koningin Astridlaan 78, Gent 9000
Tel: (09) 221 85 94 Email: pavan@pandora.be

Acknowledgments

This book would not have been possible without the contribution of the following people: The knitters, for their invaluable dedication and hard work: Dorothy Bayley, Cynthia Brent, Pat Church, Shirley Kennett, Penny Hill, Jaquie Dunt, Janet Kopinski, Maisie Lawrence, Frances Wallace. The creative and technical team: Jane Bunce for her tremendous practical and creative input and contributing the baby's kaftan. Jane Crowfoot, for her beautiful embroidery on the kaftan and shoes and the Fair Isle bag. Penny Hill for pattern compiling and providing an excellent knitter with her mother Pat Church, who also embroidered the jacket. Melody Griffiths for the lovely alphabet blanket and dressing gown. Rosy Tucker, for the cable and seed stitch jacket, and the topknot hat and socks. Sandra Lousada, not only for her beautiful photography, but also for her total commitment to this publication, which went well beyond the call of duty! Sammie Bell, the stylist, for her perfect styling and creating the look. Rosy Tucker, for her expert pattern checking, and for being such a pleasure to work with. Denise Bates at Ebury, for initating the publications and her unfailing support throughout them. Maggie Town, for the design concept of the book. Sally Harding, the editor, for pulling it all together. The models–Charlie, Ella, Iris, Joey, Kieran, Kyran, Lavinia, Molly, Lauren, Lily, Tally, Somerset, Lea. Designer Yarns, for making my yarns possible. Brandon Mably, for being a good friend. Heather Jeeves, a great agent.

WITHDRAWN